Changing the World ...

... One Book at a Time

Cindy,
a wonderful person
and a great friend. Sue
and I love you in our own
special way!
Love
and Sue

Changing the World ...

... One Book at a Time

James Parkinson

I say, there is no darkness but ignorance.
– William Shakespeare, *Twelfth Night*

Kentucky Publishing Services

Published by Kentucky Publishing Services
An imprint of the University Press of Kentucky

Editorial and Sales Offices: The University Press of Kentucky
663 South Limestone Street, Lexington, Kentucky 40508-4008
www.kentuckypress.com

Cataloging-in-Publication data available from the Library of Congress

ISBN 978-1-950690-00-8 (hardcover : alk. paper)

This book is printed on acid-free paper meeting
the requirements of the American National Standard
for Permanence in Paper for Printed Library Materials.

Manufactured in the United States of America.

Contents

The Elixir of Life

A FEW YEARS AGO, a self-help fad provocatively called "The Secret" promised untold riches and prosperity—if you'd just watch the video and read the book.

But far from being revolutionary, the message was just a new take on an old theme: the power of positive thinking. The Big Secret was really a Big Reminder.

My message isn't new either, nor is it a secret, although it does tend to get forgotten or overlooked.

Simply put, my Big Reminder is this: Education is the elixir of life.

To be literate and learned are as important and valuable as any gifts we can give to ourselves and to society.

Throughout recorded history, the positive benefits of gaining knowledge have been demonstrated over and over and over again. Knowledge is power; power is enlightenment; enlightenment is progress; progress is more knowledge.

Look at the beginning of the Renaissance. The seminal event that put an end to the Dark Ages and ushered in the modern era of Enlightenment was the invention of the printing press by Johannes Gutenberg in 1450. It is no coincidence that great breakthroughs in the sciences, the arts, medicine, exploration, human rights, literature, entertainment, even religion, rushed in tsunami-like soon after the written word became available to the masses as never before. Suddenly, it was as if the entire world began to brainstorm.

In my first book, *Autodidactic: Self-Taught,* I wrote about the importance of each of us taking responsibility for our own education. No one should ever relinquish to anyone else the great privilege it is to learn and to be literate. Nearly six hundred years since the invention of the printing press, we really have no excuse. We can free ourselves from our own Dark Ages.

In *Changing the World ... One Book at a Time* I write about all I have learned as a direct result of writing my first book, and from giving my literacy program to schools and students across America. I also share what I have learned from mentors and others with whom I have interacted in my role as an accidental academic. From teachers, students, administrators, politicians, scientists, parents, and more than a few sidewalk philosophers, I have become acutely aware of what's right and, sadly, what's lacking in our schools and our homes when it comes to literacy and learning in twenty-first–century America.

It has been quite the education.

1

Shiloh

ON A DAY ABOUT as nice as nice gets in the South, which passes for about as nice as nice gets anywhere, I crossed over the Mississippi line into Tennessee and followed the signs that pointed toward Shiloh. It is mid-April; azaleas, orchids, violets, and dogwoods are in full bloom, the countryside as green as Ireland. The rental car I'm driving is a Japanese Toyota—a reminder, apart from the calendar, that America has had many more conflicts, and differences to move beyond, than the War Between the States.

But at Shiloh, the past is always present.

On an April weekend in 1862, one of the most significant battles—if not the most significant—in U.S. history was fought along the banks of the Tennessee River. Gettysburg is more famous, Vicksburg more dramatic, Antietam more bloody, but all those Civil War battles came later, and might not have turned out the way they did—ultimately preserving the Union—if not for a battle centered around a log-cabin Methodist church the locals had named Shiloh, a Hebrew word meaning "Place of Peace."

Of the one hundred thousand soldiers who fought at Shiloh, about an equal number on each side, twenty-four thousand of them—one in four—were killed, wounded, or went missing during the two days of fighting. To that point the Civil War, already a year old, was trending strongly toward the South. Shiloh, too, appeared to be a Southern triumph after the first day, but on the second, with timely (and unexpected) Union reinforcements pouring in from eastern Tennessee, the tide turned. By nightfall Monday, only the camouflage of darkness allowed a mass of gray coats to retreat to Confederate ground and take refuge in the Mississippi crossroads town of Corinth.

As author and Civil War historian Winston Groom noted in the *New York Times,* "The significance of Shiloh cannot be overstated. If the Union had lost badly, there would have been practically nothing standing in the way of a Southern invasion."

A century and a half later, twelve hundred acres of lush forestland have been preserved at the Shiloh National Military Park. The little log church that stood at the center of the fighting still stands, renovated and open to visitors, finally a place of peace. Memorials to both Union and Confederate troops are reverently interspersed at appropriate intervals in copses of maple and hickory trees and large clearings of bluegrass bordered by Virginia pines. A cemetery with hundreds of identical head-stones, memorializing both the gray and the blue, sits languidly next to the Tennessee River. Time stands still at Shiloh, the trees and spaciousness entrapping a quiet that says there's been enough carnage here.

As I park the Toyota and walk to the Shiloh church, my thoughts turn to a Union soldier at Shiloh named Andrew Jackson Smith.

Unlike the slave-owning eighteenth president of the United States for whom he was named, Andrew Jackson Smith was neither free nor white. His mother was a slave named Susan, imprisoned on a plantation in Lyon County, Kentucky, that was owned by Elijah Smith, a man who, in addition to being a devoted fan of President Jackson, was both Andy's master and his father.

When the Civil War broke out, the Confederate Army started round-ing up young male slaves to help build its forts. When he heard the re-cruiters coming to get him, Andy jumped the fence at the edge of the Smith plantation and ran as fast as he could in the opposite direction. All through a rainy night and into the following day he fled, until he stum-bled into an army outpost, where, fortunately, everyone was wearing blue coats. The Illinois Infantry Regiment of Ulysses S. Grant's Union Army, stationed in Smithland, Kentucky, took the twenty-year-old in like a stray.

Black men were not allowed to fight in either army at the begin-ning of the Civil War, but they could enlist as servants, which is how Andy Smith came to be assigned to John Warner, a major in the Illinois Infantry Regiment. Scant weeks later, Andy Smith and John Warner found them-selves hip deep in the chaos at Shiloh, where Smith sat at the edge of a clearing and watched as a cannonball nearly cut Warner in half. Hanging onto life, the major was sent back to his home in Illinois, and Smith went along with him, dutifully attending to Warner as he recovered.

Andy Smith thus found himself in Clinton, Illinois, on January 1, 1863, when President Lincoln issued his Emancipation Proclamation, lib-erating all slaves in the South.

Andy's first decision as a free man was to join the Union Army and fight as a fully invested soldier for everything Abraham Lincoln stood for. He joined the 55th Massachusetts Infantry. By all accounts, he was a brave, fearless soldier, and never more so than at the Battle of Honey Hill in South Carolina in November 1864, where the company's flag bearer went down in the face of a ferocious frontal assault by the Confederates. Carrying the colors was an important duty, heralding to the troops following behind where to move, when to advance, when to retreat.

It was Andy Smith who rushed forward and rescued the colors that day. Holding high both the regimental and Union flags, he led the 55th Massachusetts through the worst of the carnage and ultimately out of harm's way. When the dust cleared, his commander recommended him for the Medal of Honor. (Due to a number of complications, including incomplete recordkeeping, politics, and no doubt racism, it was not awarded until 2001, when in a posthumous ceremony at the White House, President Bill Clinton bestowed Andrew Jackson Smith's Medal of Honor upon his ninety-three-year-old daughter, Caruth.)

In my mind 's eye, I can see a young Andy Smith, from Shiloh to Honey Hill, battling for rights and privileges his ancestors probably never even dared dream about—rights and privileges, for that matter, Andy Smith no doubt couldn't completely understand.

He was fighting not to be owned by another, not to be someone else's property—that was fundamental. He was fighting to be able to go where he wanted, work where he chose, live where he pleased. Equally important, if less stated and understood, he was fighting for the right to learn.

Among those things slaves were forbidden to do in the antebellum South was to learn to read and write.

Plantation owners knew only too well the problems that came with an educated workforce. The three Rs—reading, 'riting, and 'rithmetic—caused people to think about a fourth R: their rights. Knowledge was power. Rather than focusing only on plowing and picking and getting the crop in on time, gaining an education opened up limitless new horizons and possibilities. It inspired questions that demanded answers.

Before America even became America, the first formal law against slaves learning, specifically prohibiting writing, was passed in South Carolina in 1740, in response to the Cato Rebellion—named after a slave called Cato who could read and write and used the written word to call his fellow captives to insurrection. In 1800, the South Carolina law was expanded to outlaw all "mental instruction." In 1831, the Nat Turner Rebellion in Virginia was led by a literate slave, Nat Turner, who had a gift with words. His speeches and writings incited a powerful slave uprising. It left dozens dead and spurred the formalization of antiliteracy laws that were quickly passed all across the South between 1832 and 1839. In 1841, Mississippi went so far as to expel all free blacks from the state, in an effort to keep those who already knew how to read and write away from those who didn't.

"Knowledge makes a man unfit to be a slave. Once you learn to read you will be forever free," said renowned freedom fighter Frederick Douglass, whose own escape from slavery as a twenty-year-old in Maryland in 1838 was fueled by first covertly educating himself when he was a young man and then using that knowledge to foment his own rebellion and escape from tyranny.

This book isn't about race. It isn't about any creed, color, persuasion, nationality, religion, or philosophy. What it is about is education and its paramount importance to humankind as a whole and to each of us as individuals. Its core message is that the fundamentals of reading and writing are too important, too overarching, to ever be treated as selective privileges, to be doled out only to some.

The Civil War emphatically underscored that point. The war that liberated the slaves opened the floodgates of learning to all. For the first time in the nation's history, no one could be excluded from getting an education.

There is no more dramatic example in our national story about the inherent, innate desire to learn and become educated than the postwar rush by freed slaves to join the ranks of the literate, to study and learn, to send their children to school, to truly embrace the land of the free.

Andrew Jackson Smith's story is illustrative of that. Already in his mid-twenties when the war ended, and in a hurry to make up for lost opportunities, the veteran of Shiloh and hero of Honey Hill never did learn to read and write himself; family lore has it that he signed his name with an X until the day he died. Nonetheless, through sheer will and the tonic of freedom, he became one of the largest landowners in Bryan County, Kentucky, and he made certain that above all else, his two daughters, Geneva and Caruth, would get all the education they needed and more. To the point that when the girls got to sixth grade, the end of the line as far as mandatory education was concerned in Kentucky, he sent them over the border to Terre Haute, Indiana, so they could get further schooling.

I learned this bit of family history from Andrew Jackson Smith's grandson, Andrew Bowman, who lives in Indianapolis, Indiana. Andrew is in his eighties. He never met his namesake grandfather in person, but from stories he heard from his mother and his aunt, both of them "avid readers till the day they died," he knows how seriously education and literacy were stressed by their father. And he knows firsthand the high priority learning has had with the Smiths ever since.

"I'm confident my grandfather would be pleased if he came back and saw what his family was doing with education," said Andrew, a retired Federal Aviation Administration worker, who remembered a conversation he had with his son David when David was a young man.

"We were talking and I told him that at one time slaves, like his great-grandfather, were forbidden to read or write, it was against the law. He asked me, 'Why's that?' I said, 'Well, if you can read and write you can reason, and if you can reason you probably won't be a slave.' He listened to what I said and he said back to me, 'That must be awful powerful, Dad.' I said, 'It is; it's the most powerful thing you can do—to learn to read and write and comprehend.'"

Andrew Jackson Smith's great-grandson took that lesson to heart. David Smith graduated first in his chemical engineering class at Howard University before moving on to acquire his medical degree at Indiana University.

The Smith heritage is full of educated people with stories like David's, according to Sharon MacDonald, a retired professor of history at Illinois State University who is writing a biography of Andrew Jackson Smith. "Education is so important to them, so extremely important," she said. "The family is an American success story, writ large, and it goes back to a man who valued literacy and education because he didn't have it."

More than a century and a half later, the question we all need to be asking ourselves is this: do we take literacy and education for granted because we DO have it?

In an America characterized by freedom for all, where it's not against the law to learn how to read, why are so many of our children illiterate and/or alliterate? If it's not illegal, what exactly is our problem?

2

My Crusade

AFTER MY VISIT TO the Shiloh battlefield in Tennessee, I turned the car around and headed back south, where I had appointments to visit a number of high schools to talk about literacy and learning.

My first two stops were at the towns of Falkner and Ripley in the northeast part of Mississippi. Falkner is named after the great-grandfather of William Faulkner, the famed author and one of Mississippi's proudest contributions to literature (who for some reason spelled his surname with a *u,* unlike his great-grandfather). Ripley is the hometown of my good friend Wilbur Colom, a pretty famous Mississippian in his own right—and a man we'll get to know better in a later chapter.

Ever since I retired as a trial lawyer, I've had the privilege of traveling around the country, talking about the importance of literacy and education to thousands upon thousands of high school–age students, one assembly at a time. I can hardly believe my good fortune at being able to do this. As anyone who knows me will attest, I've always liked to talk, and this gives me the chance to not only talk about a subject near and dear to my heart, but with the added bonus that I don't have to worry if a jury is going to agree with me.

As I drove through the countryside, I reflected on the case that got me to this point, the big one that set me free financially so that I could become an accidental academic and spread the word about literacy and education. Appropriately enough, the case was all about the importance and the power of words.

In the mid-1990s, I was into my third decade as a trial lawyer in my hometown of Indio, California. Trial lawyers represent clients who are seeking compensation for being wronged—victims of workplace mishaps, car accidents, unscrupulous financiers, abusive employers, and so forth. Typically, the lawyer receives a percentage, usually about a third, of any compensation that is awarded. No compensation, no pay.

Fortunately, I'd won my fair share of cases during my career, succeeding in getting a number of substantial verdicts for my clients (and myself). But it was the payout from a case that became known as Big Tobacco that gave me the wherewithal to shutter my law office and embark on my literacy crusade.

A friend from law school, Tom Parry, a prominent Washington, D.C. lobbyist, helped arrange for my invitation to become part of the nationwide team of plaintiffs' lawyers involved in the tobacco litigation. The case was already well under way when I became "of counsel" to the San Diego law firm of Casey, Gerry, Reid & Schenk and the Newport Beach firm of Robinson, Calcagnie and Robinson and joined the massive suit against America's largest tobacco manufacturers who were accused of willfully deceiving the public about the health hazards of tobacco.

The allegation was that through their own research, the companies that manufactured and sold tobacco knew that nicotine and other ingredients in cigarettes, cigars, and other tobacco products were both addictive and harmful to the body. But for the obvious reason that they didn't want to reduce their revenues, they knowingly and purposely kept that information from the public.

As in all legal matters, the hard part was proving it.

The first significant breakthrough came when a Florida lawyer named Norwood "Woody" Wilner, representing a client named Gracy Carter who had smoked cigarettes for forty-three years and developed lung cancer, sued the tobacco company Brown & Williamson, claiming the company should be liable for Carter's medical expenses. In the course of his investigation, Wilner uncovered private documents written by the tobacco company that showed it was aware of the health dangers tobacco posed. The result was the first successful civil suit verdict in an American courtroom against a tobacco company.

That and other developments set the stage for the massive nationwide suit pitting the attorneys general from forty-six states against the country's four largest cigarette manufacturers, aka "Big Tobacco."

The "smoking gun" in the case came when a former tobacco industry insider, a chemist named Jeffrey Wigand, produced documents that categorically showed that not only did the industry know of tobacco's harmful properties, but it actively covered them up. Included were dozens and dozens of pages from Wigand's own personal diary he kept when he was in the employ of Brown & Williamson.

Pure and simple, it was words—the tobacco industry's own words—that resulted in the $246 billion Tobacco Master Settlement Agreement in 1998—still the largest civil litigation settlement in U.S. history.

To this day, the power of those words reverberates, and in many positive ways beyond monetary compensation. Since the Big Tobacco settlement, restrictions on tobacco advertising and aggressive antismoking campaigns funded directly by the settlement have effectively reduced smoking in America by more than 60 percent. It's incalculable to reckon how many lives have been saved and how much people's health has improved as the result of those documents and the changes they wrought.

What if the words in those documents had never been written? Worse, what if no one had bothered to read them? Worse yet, what if no one knew how to read them? It is no small stretch to suggest that the ability to read and comprehend words is the most fundamental step in acquiring the knowledge that becomes power.

I was as proud to play a small part in the case against Big Tobacco as I am to play a small part in promoting literacy and learning in America.

My first pursuit after retiring as a lawyer was to fulfill a lifelong goal of writing a book. The result was *Autodidactic: Self-Taught.* "Autodidactic" is a fancy word that, as the title suggests, simply means "self-taught." The book is partly autobiographical as it traces my own somewhat turbulent and troubled personal journey through the American education system—a story that begins with my being an indifferent student (to put it mildly) who grudgingly (and somewhat miraculously) makes his way through high school before finally beginning to appreciate how important it is for him to take responsibility for his own education. The day I realized I needed to be in charge of my own learning—no one else, not my parents, not my teachers at school, just me—made all the difference.

Looking back, I can clearly see that no matter how wonderful the teachers or how supportive the education system, if you don't make up your mind that you're going to do your part and be an active participant in your schooling, it wouldn't make any difference if you were being taught by Einstein, Plato, or Stephen Hawking!

Since my book was published in 2009, I've been able to deliver more than forty thousand copies to junior and senior high school students as I've traveled through the states of California, Utah, Indiana, New Jersey, and Mississippi to talk about literacy.

These trips have been immensely rewarding from a personal standpoint. For a person who has had no formal training as an educator but who is endlessly curious about learning, seeing the wheels of education turning up close, from the inside, is like a sports fan's getting a sideline pass to an NFL game, or getting to walk inside the ropes at a PGA golf tournament.

Teachers and administrators have welcomed me into their offices and faculty rooms with their ancient but comfortable couches and the ubiquitous coffee machines in the corner. Before and after my presentations—and this is my favorite part—students come up to talk to me one-on-one, peppering me with questions, their voices and faces full of energy and hope and curiosity. Can I really get into a college? What should I study? What's your favorite book? And, of course, How much money do you make?

As I've made my rounds of the nation's schools and distributed my little book, I've been consistently impressed by the warm reception I have received from educators. They haven't treated a curious interloper like myself—a former trial lawyer, no less—with any wariness at all. I'm welcomed with open arms. Some schools, such as the one in Falkner, Mississippi, invite all the kids to attend—every single student in the school. We had to use the gym for that one. Five hundred students in a town named for William Faulkner's great-grandfather listening to a lawyer from California talking about how great, rewarding, and important it is to read and write and learn!

3

Downward Trend

BUT IF MY TRAVELS have exposed me to the grassroots of American education in a wonderfully up-close-and-personal way, they have also exposed me to a disturbing trend that might best be illustrated by an incident that happened as I was walking across the lawn of a high school near where I live in California. I'd just finished talking to hundreds of high school students in the auditorium at Coachella Valley High and was making my way to the parking lot when two students stopped to talk to me.

I had a newspaper with me and discussed with them an article I'd just read. When I asked them to read a couple of paragraphs I'd found interesting, I made a startling discovery: they could read the words in the newspaper, but they had no idea what they meant.

These were two lively, inquisitive, energetic teenagers enrolled in an average California high school—and the newspaper flummoxed them. THEY COULD NOT READ.

Unfortunately, this was no aberration. Statistics show that Americans don't read and write nearly as much as they used to. In the land of the free and the home of the brave, our literacy percentages are going down, not up. As hard as our schools are trying, as much as technology has improved the dissemination of information, we continue to lose ground on basic reading skills.

According to the U.S. Department of Education and the National Institute of Literacy, 14 percent of the adult population in America can't read. That means people who lack the ability to recognize words on a printed page and comprehend the meaning of those words at a functional level.

The hard truth is that some thirty-three million grownup Americans are considered illiterate—a number equivalent to the entire population of Texas and Oklahoma.

It gets worse among high school graduates: 19 percent can't read at what the National Center for Educational Statistics defines as "the ability to use printed information to function in society, increase knowledge and achieve goals."

You read that right: one out of every five high school students, wearing a cap and gown and receiving their diploma on graduation day, can't read much beyond their name on the certificate.

Under the heading of "Just when you think things can't get any worse," I got an e-mail from Benjamin Heuston, the current president and CEO of Waterford Institute, informing me of the 2017 research from what is commonly called "The Nation's Report Card."

"The latest data that just came out indicate that only thirty-seven percent of our fourth graders are on grade level or above—which means we're failing sixty-three percent of our children. As I'm sure you're aware, those numbers don't get better over time—in twelfth grade it's the same thirty-seven percent that are on grade level or above (despite the many children who have dropped out of the system by that point in time). Given that our economy is increasingly knowledge-based, only having thirty-seven percent of our graduates able to fully participate in the economy is a terrible commentary on our educational system. Imagine if we had the same outcomes in medicine!"

Those two students I encountered in California are definitely not alone. And the reading problem is not limited to kids who don't plan to go on to college after high school. According to the administrators who run the ACT college entrance exam, 60 percent of students who take the test do not score sufficiently high to be considered prepped for success in college. That is why remedial English—so-called "dumbbell" English—is a course routinely offered at colleges across the country. Nationally, 11 percent of incoming college freshmen are required to take remedial English before they can move on to college-level English. Bear in mind, these are the students who have graduated from high school and decided they want to continue pursuing their education. And here's another sobering statistic: of those 11 percent, 70 percent do not go on to graduate.

"Reading is an essential component of college and workplace readiness," stated the ACT report. "Low literacy levels often prevent students from mastering other subjects. Poor readers struggle to learn in text-heavy courses and are frequently blocked from taking academically more challenging courses."

The result is more and more people emerging into the making-a-living phase of their lives without being adequately educated and prepared for success.

America is widely considered the global leader, the most powerful nation on earth, and rightly so on so many counts. But not in literacy. An international study conducted in 2013 by the Organization for Economic Co-operation and Development, of which the United States is a founding member, ranked the United States just sixteenth in literacy among a group of twenty-three developed nations, lagging far behind Japan, Finland, and the Netherlands at the top of the list.

Here are the complete rankings: 1. Japan, 2. Finland, 3. The Netherlands, 4. Australia, 5. Sweden, 6. Norway, 7. Estonia, 8. Belgium, 9. Czech Republic, 10. Slovak Republic, 11. Canada, 12. Korea, 13. United Kingdom, 14. Denmark, 15. Germany, 16. United States, 17. Austria, 18. Northern Ireland, 19. Poland, 20. Ireland, 21. France, 22. Spain, 23. Italy.

Bear in mind that being literate doesn't mean just being able to read and comprehend, it also means being able to write properly. Poor reading skills translate to poor writing skills, and vice versa.

When I was doing research for *Autodidactic,* I contacted the head of human resources for one of America's Fortune 500 companies. I had been told that all major companies receive thousands of résumés every day via the Internet, and over 75 percent of them are immediately discarded because of obvious spelling and grammatical errors. I wanted to find out if this was true. I was assured that was the case.

When I asked for examples, the HR chief sent me the following e-mail, which I have reprinted exactly as I received it—full of misspellings, misplaced words, and grammatical errors:

> Jim,
>
> I wanted to reach out to you with both an appology and some information. First, my appologies on the lateness of this getting this message to you. My original email was sitting in my drafts folder so it obviously did not get to you in midJuly as I had promised. Hopefully, the few examples that are attached to this message are helpful to you and can add to your education efforts.

I hoped he was kidding. I'm afraid he wasn't.

What does it all mean? On a worldwide scale, it means the United States is losing its edge in an increasingly flat marketplace. Here at home, it means increases in poverty, crime, and ignorance. Court statistics bear this out. According to the website BeginToRead.com, 85 percent of teenagers in the juvenile court system are illiterate, while more than 70 percent of adult inmates in U.S. prisons are unable to read above a fourth-grade level.

The numbers reveal a self-fulfilling prophecy: a lack of education and literacy reduces a person's chances of economic prosperity, too often leading quite literally to a life of crime to get by. As the Department of Justice pointed out in response to the alarming statistics cited above, "The link between academic failure and delinquency, violence, and crime is welded to reading failure."

The World Literacy Foundation estimates that illiteracy costs the United States of America over $350 billion every year due to unemployment, lack of workplace productivity, and crime.

All the while, literacy levels in America's schools continue to decline at an alarming rate. Consider Mississippi's plight. For years, the state has ranked fiftieth—that's dead last—or nearly last when comparing the quality of its education with that of the other states. Literacy levels are a particular problem.

Statistics show that year-in, year-out, 79 percent of Mississippi fourth graders do not get passing scores on national standardized reading tests. That means only two of every ten Mississippi kids moving on to fifth grade are considered proficiently literate.

In California, where literacy rates for schoolkids are also perennially near the bottom, 50 percent of the students at Coachella Valley High School fail freshmen English: 50 percent!

And yet, from personal observation and experience, I know the young people in Mississippi and California are every bit as energetic, enthusiastic, capable, and eager to learn as young people I've observed elsewhere around the country. The problem isn't in the quality of the student, the problem is the disconnect between the educational system and those it is charged with educating. The fundamental message is getting lost, and not just in Mississippi and California, but in far too many places across America.

4

The Sheer Joy of Knowing

IN HIS EXCELLENT BOOK *The Knowledge Deficit*, E. D. Hirsch, Jr. points out that to know things, you have to know things.

Knowledge doesn't come all at once, like a tidal wave; it is acquired step by step, piece by piece, in building-block fashion. One piece of information leads to more pieces of information, leading to a growing reservoir of understanding.

Merely being able to read words on a page isn't enough; they need to be understood. A frame of reference is necessary to give the words relevance and context.

"The printed text always takes something for granted, always leaves blanks to be filled in by the reader to make it comprehensible," explains Hirsch. "Unless writers and their readers internalize the shared knowledge of the wider speech community, they cannot expect the blanks to be filled in; they cannot be successful writers or proficient readers."

When we read, we fill in a lot of unstated connections. Most of the time we don't even realize we're doing it. Hirsch asks us to consider the following sentence as an example: "Jones sacrificed and knocked in a run." If you're an American who likes sports, you'll no doubt understand what's being communicated because the language of baseball will be a part of your knowledge background. You'll know that in baseball a sacrifice means making an out in order to drive in a run for your team. But what if you're from England or Ireland, where they don't play much baseball? You'll read those words and even though they're in English, you won't have a clue what's being said.

Effective learning doesn't take place in a vacuum. The greater our knowledge background, the more we can learn. The more we learn, the more we can relate; the more we can relate, the more we can learn.

Educators who understand this create courses of study that are broad and well rounded, not skipping any steps or subjects.

"Gains in reading are directly proportional to the completeness with which a school implements a coherent, content-rich curriculum," Hirsch writes. "A system of specific content standards coupled with curriculum-based tests will cause achievement on non-curriculum-based tests to rise over time. It will result in higher achievement overall and a narrowing of the academic gap between rich and poor."

In other words, a well-rounded education helps counteract any disadvantages of who you're born to and where you live.

The benefits of all this learning? Better grades, better jobs, better security. Those are the obvious practical ones, of course. But beyond that, there's the intrinsic value of just knowing.

Being educated makes the walk of life so much more interesting and enjoyable. There is immense, incalculable joy in learning, in exercising our minds, in experiencing the thrill of discovery, in exclaiming, "I didn't know that!" It's knowledge that makes life compelling, a never-ending puzzle to be assembled. It is the spice of great conversation, the source of spirited discussion and debate, the entryway to countless worlds full of fascinating people and philosophy and information.

I believe we are all hard-wired to learn, that the desire to be educated is intrinsic in all of us. I recently watched an episode of *The Crown* on television. It featured a young Queen Elizabeth, just learning the ropes of being queen of England, suddenly having to meet with Prime Minister Winston Churchill and other politicians and dignitaries. She found it frustrating not to be able to talk with these worldly men about much more than the weather and the food they were eating for lunch. Because she was a member of the royalty, her schooling had been restricted to learning about royal things: proper etiquette, how to behave at a state dinner, which fork to use for the first course of a meal, how to dress and bow and curtsy, those sorts of things. She was exempted from learning about current affairs and politics and other subjects considered too mundane and unnecessary for a queen-in-waiting.

"Why?" Elizabeth wails to her mother. Why wasn't she taught the same things as ordinary kids—so she could have a decent conversation with others?

Her mother explains that Elizabeth knew all she needed to know for her special role, but Elizabeth isn't having it. She hires a tutor to come to Buckingham Palace and school her about math and science and world affairs. Even queens, especially queens, want to be in the know.

5

A Leaky System

SO WHY AM I picking on the education system in America. Could the system possibly be an impediment to literacy and learning?

There's nothing wrong, of course, with the fundamental premise American education rests upon: that our schools are available to everyone, no exceptions. That's the goal. The notion of education for all is America's shining beacon to the world. That's our rock.

But if the goal is sound, the implementation is flawed and getting more so. By any objective measurement, education has gotten significantly worse in America over the years.

Whenever I talk to foundations about sponsoring either my literacy campaign or other education initiatives, they talk about wanting to see proof that the program works—they want it to be evidence based. But if they had really applied that standard over the past sixty years, no programs would have been funded. Why? Because they all failed. How could you possibly have evidence that they succeeded when education hasn't improved, it's regressed?

Time and again, the system keeps getting hijacked by fads, trends, gimmicks, and, worst of all, bureaucracy.

Diane Ravitch knows that bureaucracy well. She is one of America's most respected authorities on education. She earned her PhD in the history of education from Columbia. Two presidents, George H. W. Bush and Bill Clinton, appointed her to public office: she served as Assistant Secretary of Education during both of their administrations. Over the years, she's written no less than twenty-one books about education. She knows the country's education system inside and out and has seen it through many twists and turns.

In 2010, she wrote a bestselling book with the provocative title *The Death and Life of the Great American School System: How Testing and Choice Are Undermining Education.*

In the book, Ravitch, who once championed federally mandated testing in schools and the array of choices offered in the burgeoning charter-school era, reverses field, disavowing her previous views. The reason? It all looked good on paper, but the reforms that once appeared so promising took on a different hue after they had been implemented. She writes: "I have concluded that most of the reform strategies that school districts, state officials, the Congress, and federal officials are pursuing, that mega-rich foundations are supporting, and that editorial boards are applauding are mistaken. These policies are corrupting educational values."

In the beginning, when plans were being formulated for No Child Left Behind and other programs that would standardize testing and then hold schools' and teachers' feet to the fire based on the results of those tests, Ravitch admits she was swept up in the fever of possibilities, joining others with high expectations:

> I too had fallen for the latest panaceas and miracle cures; I too had drunk deeply of the elixir that promised a quick fix to intractable problems. I too had jumped aboard a bandwagon, one festooned with banners celebrating the power of accountability, incentives, and markets. I too was captivated by the ideas that promised to end bureaucracy, to ensure that poor children were not neglected, to empower poor parents, to enable poor children to escape failing schools, and to close the achievement gap between rich and poor, black and white. Testing would shine a spotlight on low-performing schools, and choice would create opportunities for poor kids to leave for better schools. All of this seemed to make sense, but there was little empirical evidence, just promise and hope. I wanted to share the promise and hope.

Alas, time did not support the lofty predictions. To the contrary, things only got worse. School choice and standardized testing didn't level the playing field; they tilted it even more. The gap between rich and poor, privileged and oppressed, effectively educated and woefully undereducated only widened. It turned out that placing the emphasis on testing made the test, not the learning, the end-all. The students' aptitude actually declined, and that wasn't conjecture. Test scores proved it!

At that, the woeful test results don't tell how bad it really is, because of the amount of cheating that goes on due to the stress the testing puts on both teachers and pupils to perform.

When I give my literacy talk to schools, I ask every student in the room to close their eyes. I then ask anyone who's cheated this year to raise their hand. I've done this exercise across the country and, without fail, 99 percent of the hands go up.

Later, when I'm alone with the faculty, I'll ask them to close their eyes and raise their hands if they ever helped a student cheat on those all-important statewide tests. Unfortunately, many hands go up here too.

(And it doesn't stop with high school. Kim Clark is the current commissioner of education for the Latter-day Saints Church. Before that, he was dean of the Harvard Business School. During a round of golf, Kim told me that the first year they interviewed applicants to HBS they discovered that over one third of the applicants did not write their own essays. Keep in mind, these were the top three hundred applicants as measured by grade point averages and GMAT scores. The top of the top. Yet a third of them didn't feel their own writing skills could get them into Harvard. So they cheated. My friends in academia tell me this phenomenon is not limited to Harvard but is found in every school in America).

Creating stress is just one way that reforms, fads, quick fixes, and gimmicks are so often counterproductive. Typically, they are the product of a bureaucracy, mandated from above, the outcome of committee meetings and groupthink far removed from the classroom—innovations from people eager to justify their own existence. In theory they should be transformative; in practice, they impede more than they improve.

It's not new. I remember the great debate over how to teach reading in California when I was a kid. One side favored phonics—sounding out the word. The other side favored teaching reading by sight—you saw the whole word and you said it. The superintendent of schools, a man named Bill Honig, sided with whole word, so that's what was taught. That's how I learned. Then, thirty years later, Bill Honig changed his mind and decided whole word was wrong and phonics was right, so it was back to the drawing board. This mess still hasn't been figured out (although the experimental evidence favors phonics).

Everyday Math is a well-known recent example of a reform managing to create more problems than it solves. Scholars at the University of

Chicago spent thirteen years developing a new way to teach elementary kids math, replacing traditional arithmetic with more creative ways to teach addition, subtraction, division, and multiplication. While this reform math was praised by a few—mostly those who conceived of it—it was roundly criticized by many, many others. An article in *Forbes* typified the discontent: "Complaints are widespread that it is confounding for parents and children. And it doesn't build on concepts or scaffold understanding. It has children learn 2 plus 2 in 500 different ways."

Hundreds of top mathematicians from around the country petitioned the Secretary of Education not to endorse the program. Mandated to try the new approach, California revised its Everyday Math textbooks, while the state of Texas banned the curriculum altogether, on the grounds that it wasn't preparing students for college. And yet, Everyday Math has not been totally abandoned; far from it. It is left to flounder, trying to justify the years of research spent to produce it.

Typically, the new and innovative programs come from the top down, the product of education elites who tell the people in the classrooms what to implement, as opposed to asking the people in the classrooms what they want and what works.

There seems to be no end to the tinkering. In 2001, President George W. Bush's administration pushed through Congress the No Child Left Behind Act, a bill that linked the amount of federal funds schools could receive to standardized annual testing. That one proved so ineffective it was replaced in 2015 by the Every Student Succeeds Act, a program that ostensibly gives more control to the states, yet still involves federally mandated testing.

In between NCLB and ESSA, in 2009 the Obama administration created Race to the Top, a program that pits school against school in competition for $4.35 billion in federal grant money. Schools that exhibit the most innovation and reform win the largest grants. Here, too, standardized testing is involved to determine who gets the money.

What's the result of all this testing? In California and Mississippi, I've talked to educators who have told me that they spend fifteen to twenty days every year administering standardized federal tests. That's three to four entire weeks out of a thirty-six–week school year. By the time a student graduates, they will have spent one year of their twelve years of schooling taking federal tests.

Not only do these tests determine how much funding a school will receive, but tests play a role in whether teachers and principals will be promoted or even keep their jobs and, in some cases, whether a school will continue to exist at all.

With that much at stake, it should come as no surprise that cheating scandals have resulted. The U.S. Government Accountability Office reported in 2013 that no less than forty states had reported cheating allegations in the previous two years. Among the most egregious examples of widespread cheating occurred in Atlanta, where investigators concluded that nearly two hundred educators in more than forty public schools had participated in organized cheating, going so far as shouting out answers to questions during testing, making sure low-performing students were seated next to high-performing peers so they could copy their work, and, when all that failed, getting together on weekends to change students' answers. Nine of the most serious abusers were sentenced to jail terms, some for as long as seven years.

Too often, systems and programs get in the way of the very thing they're trying to improve. Everyday Math. Phonics. No Child Left Behind. Race to the Top. Merit Pay. Smaller Classrooms. Charter Schools. Vouchers. So many new and innovative programs, so much debate, so many reforms and changes, and yet at the end of the day, education in America isn't moving the needle up, but down.

"Our national infatuation with fads, movements and reforms contributes to our collective detriment," writes Diane Ravitch. "because they invariably distract us from the steadiness of purpose needed to improve our schools."

My thinking is that teachers and schools should be encouraged to experiment in their own classrooms and see what works and what doesn't. In other words, build the driveway before you build the highway. Test in a place where if you fail it will not cost you a fortune and cause the entire operation to go bust.

When my partners and I went to Tanzania in Africa a few years ago to build a hotel, we started small, doing a little at a time, knowing if one approach didn't work, we would be able to regroup and survive. At the same time, we watched a group of Russians come into Kenya, which borders Tanzania, and buy a huge tract of land and start a $100 million housing project. The operation was so massive that when one aspect of it started to fail, everything collapsed. The houses never were built.

That is typical with a top-down deal.

As far as I'm concerned, the Department of Education should work on getting federal dollars back to local places and stay away from what's being taught in the classroom. Washington, D.C. is too far away from what's going on in classrooms to be effective.

6

Losing Ground

WHILE OPINIONS ABOUT EDUCATION are bound to forever vary and defy consensus, there is no disagreement that the very best place to ignite and launch a love of learning is in the home. There is simply no substitute for a stable home environment in fostering curiosity and a thirst for knowledge.

And the earlier the better.

Of the many studies on the subject, the one conducted by the team of University of Kansas psychologists Betty Hart and Todd Risley is the most cited and illuminating. In an exhaustive study in the 1980s, Hart and Ridley spent more than three years documenting the number of words spoken in the homes of forty-two families in the Kansas City area. Fourteen of the families were labeled as homes of professionals, fourteen were in the middle-class, wage-earner range, and fourteen were in the welfare class.

The researchers discovered that children in the welfare homes heard, per hour, an average of 616 words, children in middle-class homes an average of 1,251 words, and children of professionals an average of 2,153 words.

By the age of four, poorer kids had been exposed to 13 million words, middle-class kids to 26 million words, and professional-class kids to 45 million words. The gap between low and high: 32 million words!

Perhaps even more illuminating in the Hart and Risley study was their finding that after four years, the average child from a professional home received 560,000 more instances of positive feedback than negative feedback. For a working-class child, the difference between positive and negative was 100,000. But children in welfare homes heard, on average, 125,000 more instances of negative feedback than positive.

The study helped launch a number of government programs aimed at helping lower-income families with their children's early education, because the takeout from the Hart and Risley study is unmistakable: early nurturing is a significant and important factor in preparing children for a life of learning.

Then, too, there are the summer-slide statistics. Numerous studies have been conducted that confirm that on average students during summer vacation will forget 25 percent of what they learned during the school year. It takes six weeks in the fall to catch up to where they were in the spring.

But these same studies show that children who read books during the summer and have their brains stimulated in other educational ways show much less of a summer slide than children who don't. As you'd suspect, the studies show in addition that it's the kids from more stable, higher socioeconomic homes who are more likely to read and remain academically stimulated during the summer—giving them that much more of a head start when the next school year begins.

The Hart and Risley and Summer Slide studies are just two of many that suggest Daniel Patrick Moynihan was onto something when he came out with the Moynihan Report way back in 1965. At the time, Moynihan, later a U.S. senator from New York, was President Lyndon Baines Johnson's Assistant Secretary of Labor. As part of LBJ's War on Poverty, Moynihan was asked by the president to conduct research into the roots and reasons of black poverty in the United States.

In his report, Moynihan pointed to statistics that showed 25 percent of black children were born out of wedlock and raised in single-parent homes. His report concluded that the decline of the traditional two-parent nuclear family was the reason for escalating poverty among black people, and if the rising rate of nonnuclear family units continued unabated, poverty would only get worse. This news, perhaps predictably, was greeted with controversy and cries of racism.

Fast-forward more than fifty years, and Moynihan's findings are now praised as accurate and prescient. Today, the number of out-of-wedlock births in the black community is 72 percent, while the percentage among whites, which was 3 percent in 1965, is 29 percent—higher than it was for blacks in Moynihan's report.

This isn't to suggest that children from single-parent families can't succeed. They can, and many do.

But the question is, what policy is in the nation's best interest? This issue was publicly debated during the first Bush administration. Unfortunately, the debate was between the scriptwriters for a Hollywood sitcom starring a single mother named Murphy Brown and a vice president who couldn't spell the word potato.

It is time for another national debate.

While the trend is disturbing, understanding the causes and effects can also be the answer. America's kids, no matter who gives birth to them, need to be exposed early and often to words, reading, learning, and vocabulary. The formula is incontrovertible: laying a proper foundation when a child is young produces an enthusiasm for learning.

I can hear parents out there scoffing. Hah! My kid has no interest in school even though I loved school, talk to him all the time, and support education to the hilt! I could cite my own experience and add it to that chorus. I came from a stable, two-parent home with all the encouragement I could ask for. Both my parents graduated from college. My father was a physician. I'd bet by the time I was four I'd heard way more than 45 million words. Our home was littered with books. As early as I can remember, there was no doubt that my three brothers and I were expected to go to college and become doctors, just like my dad. (My rebellion later on, such as it was, was to become a lawyer instead.)

Yet as a youngster, I could not have cared less about education. To call me indifferent about books and learning would be giving me way too much credit. I was much more interested in playing and goofing off. By the time I got to high school, it was girls and sports.

But underlying all my antipathy was the nurturing and preparing I had received. The foundation was there for me even though I was unaware of it and did my best to ignore it. In spite of my own worst efforts, I was lucky.

The problem is, for too many of America's children, the foundation either is not there, or it is slipping fast.

7

The Good News

AFTER SPENDING FOUR CONSECUTIVE chapters dwelling on the deterioration of education in America, one might get the impression I see little hope for the future. But au contraire. While it's true that the statistics decidedly trace a steady decline of literacy and learning, we remain the greatest and most resilient country in the world—one that has proven time and time again the ability to rebound from seemingly insurmountable difficulties and rally to overcome the gloomiest of forecasts.

That's because America is made up of Americans, and as history has shown, when the country is sliding in the wrong direction, it is individual Americans who recognize the problems, step up, and turn things around.

Beyond exposing me to the deficiencies of an education bureaucracy that if not broken is certainly breaking, traveling to schools across the country has also happily opened my eyes to the remarkable individuals within the system who are achieving significant results and producing positive changes, in many cases one school and one student at a time.

These are the people who restore positivity to my cynicism, who turn my discouragement into encouragement. America might not have the greatest educational system ever invented—and whoever said educating a hundred million people was going to be easy?—but in my view the country's educators are second to none.

As I've toured rich schools and poor schools, large schools and small schools, city schools and rural schools, I've come across only one teacher who I thought didn't care. One individual who it seemed to me was just going through the motions, stumbling through the halls just trying to get through the day and pick up their paycheck. Everyone else I've met—and there have been hundreds of teachers and administrators—has given off the exact opposite impression: they care. They really, truly care. If anything, I think sometimes they might even care too much; but that is their only fault.

Our education system is packed full of remarkable human beings. In the following chapters I'd like to introduce you to some of these individuals who have impressed me and given me hope for the future. I think they'll impress you and give you hope as well.

8

The Innovator

ON A WARM, WINDSWEPT afternoon, as I stood on the farthest western point of the African continent, gazing out at the vastness of the Atlantic Ocean, a feeling of true evil overcame me.

I was standing on Gorée Island, a tiny bit of land a short ferry ride from Dakar, the capital city of the country of Senegal. It was here that the slave trade once flourished—here, at the tip of Gorée Island, where freight ship after freight ship set off for the Americas, crammed with human cargo to be bought and sold like sheep and cattle.

I visited the holding cells in the House of Slaves where the captives waited until their ship came in. I looked in horror at the Door of No Return, the portal through which millions walked toward the Atlantic and lives of bondage and abuse, never again to see their homeland or freedom.

The only thing that kept me from going into the abyss of depression was remembering why I'd come to Senegal to begin with.

It was to help the people learn to read.

I was an emissary of Dr. Dusty Heuston, a genuinely selfless and innovative educator. Because of business and professional contacts I had previously developed in Africa, Dusty had solicited my help in arranging a face-to-face meeting with the president of Senegal, Abdoulaye Wade, to explore ways to help Senegalese children with their education.

Meeting and getting to know Dusty Heuston was the first of what has amounted to a continuous string of relationships I have forged with amazing and inspiring educators ever since I launched my second "career" as an accidental academic.

The ink was barely dry on the first copies of *Autodidactic* when I met Dusty. My brother Rick made the introduction. Rick's children attended Waterford, a private school in Salt Lake City affiliated with Dusty's non-profit Waterford Research Institute. Impressed by the school's programs and seeing similarities between some of my views on self-education and the Waterford curriculum, Rick called me in California and suggested Dr. Heuston and I ought to get together.

As soon as we hung up, I made the call.

I explained to Dr. Heuston, who has an MA in American Literature from Stanford and a PhD in English Literature from New York University, my zeal for developing a program that would encourage young people to take charge of their own education.

He interrupted me.

He said, "You're talking about helping one kid at a time, right?"

"Yes, that's correct," I answered.

"I don't have any interest in that," he said.

The response wasn't unpleasant—Dusty Heuston is one of the world's nicest, kindest men—but it was adamant.

His entire focus, he informed me, was on the many, not the one.

That intrigued me. I asked if he might ever find time to meet in person, I'd love to sit down and have a long talk.

"I'm free tomorrow," he said.

"I'll be there," I answered.

I flew to Salt Lake City the next morning and made my way to Waterford's headquarters. Dusty got right to the point. Relying on teaching models that involved one teacher standing in front of a handful of students was outdated, he said, and as the world's population continued to grow was becoming more and more unsustainable.

What education needed to do was take advantage of new inventions and technologies for effectively reaching students—and not by the hundreds or thousands, but by the millions.

As a parallel, he pointed to the changing ways humankind has dug holes.

At first, people dug with their hands, which was fine until they figured out they could do it better and faster with a shovel. Then the shovel was replaced by a steam engine, then a backhoe, and so forth.

He spoke in the same vein about communication. Back in the 1800s, if you wanted to get a letter from one side of the country to the other, the quickest way was by Pony Express. Riders on horseback changing mounts every ten or fifteen miles could get mail across the country in less than twenty days. With faster horses and better saddles, the speed increased. But then in 1861, the telegraph was connected, and within two days the

Pony Express was out of business and you never heard of it again—because somebody came up with something that was infinitely better.

As advances in technology expanded exponentially from 1980 onward, any skepticism that existed in 1976 about Dusty's ideas of using computer technology to improve education disappeared as rapidly as the Pony Express.

He then proceeded to explain in detail the interactive-computer-software applications Waterford has developed that make it possible for any kid anywhere, no matter how remote or underprivileged, to learn to read and gain a quality education.

Through technology, time and distance disappear. A teacher physically standing in Manhattan can also be virtually standing inside a grass hut in Tahiti—and, with the right software, be able to interact equally with students in both places.

"It is possible to give a child the best education in every setting," said Dusty. "The speed of light takes this anywhere."

The key to it all is the interaction. One-way education—a teacher merely lecturing with no feedback—isn't nearly as effective as a lively and continuous back-and-forth and give-and-take. Learning requires a two-way street. Reading a book teaches only so much. It's when you make sure that you comprehend what you have read that you obtain real knowledge.

Dusty has a name for his interactive software: "The Third Source." In 2011, he published a book by that title—*The Third Source: A Message of Hope for Education.* He allowed me to help review and edit the book, and my name is next to his on the cover.

Based on the theory that children need to be stimulated early, Waterford's interactive software focuses on ages three through eight—no matter what their circumstances or where they might reside. As an article in *EdTech Digest* put it, "Software overcomes so many infrastructure obstacles—the bricks and mortar of the schoolhouse, teachers, travel—and connects with children wherever there's a computer."

Nearly four decades and $145 million have gone into the research and development of Waterford's curriculum, including these four pioneering programs:

- Waterford Early Reading Program: Provides a complete language-arts program for preschool through second-grade students, covering crucial skills like phonemic awareness, phonics, text comprehension, vocabulary, print concepts, readiness skills, writing, and oral fluency.

- Waterford Early Math and Science: Provides comprehensive instruction in the five major areas of early math: numbers and operation, geometry, algebra, measurement, and data analysis. The integrated science curriculum emphasizes exploration and the scientific method while teaching earth, life, and physical science.
- Camp Consonant: A multisensory tutoring program designed to help children build the most basic literacy skills. The curriculum is designed as a remediation support for children who struggle to make progress within the Waterford Early Reading Program.
- UPSTART: A pioneering, in-home kindergarten-readiness service for preschool for four-year-olds that provides the three software programs noted above plus offers personalized family support with a representative who follows up with the child's parent or guardian with progress updates and tips for creating an academically rich home environment. Each annual UPSTART cohort begins with an in-person student pre-assessment and parent orientation and ends with a post-assessment and program graduation ceremony. In Utah, legislative action has made the program widely available as a free offering to families.

These programs are being used to aid teachers and students in thousands of U.S. schools and tens of thousands of U.S. homes. Waterford's early intervention is especially effective in stepping in and helping kids who are already falling behind in the early grades. In an era when as many as 33 percent of fourth graders aren't reading at grade level, that's important.

The potential for children in places like Africa, where teachers are few and books are a rarity, is mind-boggling. With interactive technology, children in remote villages can have the same advantages as their counterparts halfway around the world.

The challenge, of course, is having technology available anywhere.

Hence, my visit to Senegal. President Wade assembled a staff of his educators, and we visited villages Waterford hoped to use as examples of the effectiveness and the reach of its innovative software. Alas, soon after my visit, President Wade left office, and the new regime put the projected program on hold.

Cutting down on the costs is a challenge, but there's no arguing that

Dusty's vision is sound. Here is a man who has an answer to the vexing problem of how to get to the underprivileged child who has not been read to by a mother or a father and who has not heard the 45 million words that a privileged kid has been able to hear before the age of four. He has been able to come up with an algorithm to get reading to the masses, with an emphasis on the critical ages of three through eight. And because of the funding he's gotten from the state of Utah, he's been able to prove that what he's doing works.

This is the only evidence-based program that I've encountered in my journey across the country to look at educational ideas.

What Waterford has accomplished in the United States so far is impressive, and small implementations of the program have also touched children in India, China, Israel, Romania, Rwanda, Senegal, Ghana, Kenya, and Taiwan.

I hope it's just the beginning.

People like Dusty Heuston show how valuable and effective grassroots educational initiatives led by altruistic people can be. His story reminds me of Andrew Carnegie.

To many people today, "Carnegie" is the name on the concert hall in New York City. But Carnegie Hall is just a small part of it.

Andrew Carnegie loved to read—and he wanted everyone else to love to read too.

Before he became the richest man in the world—when he retired in 1900 at age sixty-six his fortune was worth half a billion dollars ($13 billion today)—he had been a penniless immigrant from Scotland.

His big breakthrough came when he got a job in Pittsburgh, working for the telegraph company, and his employer, a wealthy and educated man named James Anderson, allowed his employees to use the private library in his home.

It was books and learning how to read them that Andrew Carnegie said opened up the world for him. Once he knew what was out there, there was no stopping him.

Believing that everyone should have the same opportunity, after he retired as a railroad and steel magnate, he set about giving away much of his fortune for the building of libraries (and the occasional concert hall).

In his autobiography, Carnegie explained why: "It was from my own early experience," he wrote, "that I decided there was no use to which money could be applied so productive of good to boys and girls who have good within them and ability and ambition to develop it, as the founding of a public library in a community."

By the time of his death in 1919, he had helped finance no less than 1,689 public libraries in cities and towns from one end of America to the other.

The vast majority of Carnegie's libraries are still standing today. There's simply no way to calculate just how many boys and girls have benefited.

And now, a hundred years later, technology can open the world to so many more.

9

The Learner

ON AN UNEXPECTED TRIP to Chicago, I booked my ticket from Los Angeles at the last minute and found myself in a middle seat in a middle row: an airliner's version of purgatory (especially for someone who is six foot four). Resigned to a tedious, cramped four hours in the air, I put my head down and read my book, not looking to my left or my right until they announced we were beginning our descent. That's when I noticed that the man to my right next to the window was reading a copy of *Golf Digest*. I'm ready and willing to talk about golf to anyone, anywhere, at any time, so I made an offhand comment about golf—and that's how I came to make the acquaintance of one of the world's foremost authorities on learning.

In addition to being a serious golfer, Dr. Robert Bjork, I discovered, is a psychologist. He got his doctorate at Stanford and has dedicated his career to studying how people learn. His credentials speak to the esteem in which he is held among his peers. He is Distinguished Research Professor in the Department of Psychology at UCLA, past president of the Association for Psychological Science, past editor of both *Memory & Cognition* and *Psychological Review,* and a fellow of the American Academy of Arts and Sciences, among other honors. When he's not running things at UCLA, he is an adviser, along with his wife, Elizabeth, a distinguished psychologist in her own right, to Lasting Learning, LLC (lastinglearning.com)—a Web-based community of the world's foremost learning scientists.

That's whom I found myself sitting next to. I casually asked Dr. Bjork if he'd ever written any articles. A question that, in retrospect, was like asking Jack Nicklaus if he'd ever won any golf tournaments. He looked at me like I was a freshman from rural America sitting in the back row of his psychology class. "Yes," he said. He'd written a few articles. I asked if he'd be kind enough to send me a sampling. Sure enough, a day or two later he e-mailed me about four hundred pages of material—a small sampling of the academic articles he has published. After I read all that he had e-mailed, I sent him back ten pages of questions. To that he wrote that after sending materials to people he'd sat next to on airplanes for the past thirty-five years, I was the first one who'd actually responded! A friendship was born.

But it wasn't until I received an invitation to a two-day conference called a Festschrift at UCLA honoring Dr. Bjork that I began to fully appreciate the academic world he lives in and all that he has accomplished. (A Festschrift is a celebration in writing of the academic accomplishments of a scholar. At the event, which led to a book entitled *Successful Remembering and Successful Forgetting: A Festschrift in Honor of Robert A. Bjork,* numerous colleagues, students, and friends—all top people in their fields—came together to pay tribute to Dr. Bjork's work, produce a book containing their cumulative viewpoints, and discuss current research on human memory.)

To give you an example of the depth of his thinking, here is what Dr. Bjork had to say on the topic of "Desirable Difficulties Perspective on Learning":

> Instructors and students alike are susceptible to assuming that conditions of instruction that enhance performance during instruction are the same conditions that enhance long-term learning. That assumption, however, is sometimes dramatically wrong: Manipulations that speed the rate of acquisition during instruction can fail to support long-term retention and transfer, whereas other manipulations that appear to introduce difficulties and slow the rate of acquisition learner can enhance post-instruction recall and transfer. Such manipulations, labeled desirable difficulties by the author, include spacing rather than massing study opportunities; interleaving rather than blocking practice on separate topics; varying how to-be-learned material is presented; providing intermittent, rather than continuous, feedback; and using tests, rather than presentations, as learning events. That learning profits from contending with such difficulties provides a valuable perspective on how humans learn.

My son Matt and I were able to attend several of the workshops and presentations—the only nonscholars in attendance. It's an experience we won't forget.

A few months later, Dr. Bjork invited me to come to UCLA and listen to a presentation he was giving to the law school about how we learn and how his research might fit into the law school's curriculum. To my surprise, he asked me if I had any questions or observations for the group. So I called on an evidence professor and asked her how her students learn evidence. The question stumped her. She knew how she taught her students, but it turned out she really had no clear answer for how they actually learn.

Her lack of an answer didn't surprise me, as a former law student myself. Law schools typically use the Socratic Method, using questions and argument as a way to arrive at (hopefully) a logical conclusion. Maybe some find such an adversarial approach helpful, but I know it kept me on my heels throughout law school. I was way more worried about not knowing the answer (which happened all too frequently) than absorbing knowledge. And I know I wasn't alone. Law school was about survival, not about substance. It was fear of flunking out that motivated me, not a thirst for learning.

Looking back, as a law student, did I know how to study effectively and learn the law? I did not. And the professors had no idea how their students learned the law. It was the quintessential blind leading the blind, together stumbling to the finish line.

Bjork's research challenges many accepted and preconceived notions of learning. His findings can be amazingly eye opening. A 2010 article that quoted him extensively in the *New York Times*—with the provocative headline "Forget What You Know about Good Study Habits"—was at the time the most downloaded article in the newspaper's history.

Many common teaching methods are completely backward of what they could and should be. Take testing in schools as an example. Studies show that tests should be used to help students learn, not determine what they have learned. But the role of the nationally standardized tests that are routinely administered across the nation is to grade the students, and their teachers and schools, and then move on. You either passed or you flunked and that's it. There is no follow-up, no effort to help anyone learn from their wrong answers—that is, their mistakes. The emphasis following the testing should be on what still needs to be learned and focusing on that. But it is just the opposite.

I learned from Dr. Bjork that there are good and not-so-good ways to attain and retain knowledge. Reading a chapter over and over, for instance, isn't nearly as effective as reading the chapter once and then testing yourself by writing a series of questions on three-by-five cards and seeing how well you can answer them. Repeat that process until you're satisfied you've mastered the material.

As I wrote in *Autodidactic,* when I spent two years in Argentina as a young man on a Mormon mission and needed to learn Spanish to be able to communicate, I discovered for myself the effectiveness of the three-by-five card system. Every day when I heard a word I didn't know—and there were plenty of them in the beginning—I would look up the definition in my pocket dictionary, and before I went to bed I would write down the words I'd learned on a three-by-five card along with their definitions. As I fell asleep, I'd quiz myself on the words. In that way, I learned to speak and understand conversational Spanish in a relatively short period. After that, I used the same method to expand my vocabulary to include words from newspapers and textbooks, until I felt confident in speaking Spanish. To this day, I routinely quiz myself in Spanish so I won't lose what I learned when I was in my twenties.

Another thing Dr. Bjork's research teaches us about learning: doing the same thing over and over again is not nearly as effective as changing things up. The practice is called interleaving. It means you study algebra for half an hour, then Spanish for half an hour, English for half an hour, science for half an hour, and so on. For the brain, it seems, a change is as good as a rest.

Interleaving works well for all kinds of learning, Dr. Bjork told me. He used golf as an example. When you're practicing at the driving range, you should vary the clubs you're hitting. Hit a couple of wedges, then a couple of five-irons, then a couple of drivers, and so forth, and you will achieve better results.

The point of the research of Dr. Bjork and his colleagues is that there are effective ways to learn and there are not-so-effective ways to learn. That's a valuable thing to know individually, but imagine if the education system as a whole spent its time and energy concentrating on the science of learning instead of on standardized tests that create more stress than results.

Meeting Bob Bjork literally changed the way I look at how I learn, and how I look at learning. He opened to me a vast new world of understanding. I have since read dozens of books written by him and other leaders in the field, Daniel Schacter of Harvard, Carol Dweck of Stanford, Thad Polk of the University of Michigan, Tim Lee at McMaster University, and Mark Guadagnoli of the University of Nevada-Las Vegas among them.

I found it interesting that Dr. Bjork went to college on an Evans scholarship—a grant-in-aid that's given to caddies in golf. So golf is what launched his career in academia and what launched our friendship. In the spring of 2018 I was asked to give a talk at the annual Interdisciplinary Conference on Human Performance (ICHP), an organization that Bob belongs to that includes twenty-four of the top cognitive, motor-skills, and cognitive-neuroscience researchers in the world. Once a year, alternating between the East Coast and the West Coast, they meet for two mornings of academic programs. In the afternoons, they play golf. Appropriately enough, I found myself on a golf course at Borrego Springs, California, an hour and fifteen minutes from my house, getting to talk about my literacy program and rub shoulders with these accomplished cognitive scientists (and avid golfers) who are doing incredible research and expanding humankind's capacity for learning. All because of a serendipitous meeting on an airplane.

10

The Teacher

I AM NO STRANGER to greatness. Along with Lee Benson, in 2012, I co-authored a biography of the legendary golfer Billy Casper, *The Big Three and Me*. Spotting a golfing great is easy—just go to the record book. Billy Casper is a perfect case in point: fifty-one victories on the PGA Tour, five Vardon Trophies for low stroke average, three major championships, and the most Ryder Cup points of any American golfer in history.

There is, however, no record book you can consult to determine a great teacher.

The only way to spot a great teacher is if you go to the classroom and actually watch them yourself, and then interview their students.

I did just that at Oakcrest High School in May's Landing, New Jersey.

Doug Cervi is a history teacher at Oakcrest High. He'd contacted me about using a book I wrote about World War II as part of a course he was teaching about the war. Mr. Cervi is one of those teachers who think so far outside the box there is no box. He will go to the end of the earth for his students, no matter the effort or the cost. It's all about the kids. As he likes to say in his Jersey brogue, "Teaching's the only job where you steal stuff from home and take it to work."

His approach to education is an all-out offensive. He brings history to life. Often quite literally. When he teaches about the Holocaust, he brings in a Holocaust survivor as a specially invited guest lecturer. When he's talking about the historic *Brown v. Board of Education* Supreme Court ruling, he brings in a lawyer who participated in the case. When the subject is World War II, he brings in a veteran. He's annexed a room next to his classroom as a museum to house artifacts, mementos, and objects brought by his invited guests who donate them to his cause.

We became acquainted because he read in a California newspaper about a World War II veteran I'd represented in a lawsuit brought by former World War II prisoners of war against the Japanese companies that used them as slave laborers. The case ended up being rejected by the U.S. Supreme Court because of a provision in a 1951 peace treaty between the United States and Japan that the justices deemed exonerated the Japanese companies from damages. As with the Big Tobacco case, the verdict came down to words and their interpretation.

The case was my last big fight as a trial lawyer. It introduced me to an extraordinary caliber of men who had fought so gallantly for America in World War II. Despite losing the case, friendships and relationships remained, and I ended up coauthoring a book with Lee Benson about the case called *Soldier Slaves* that was later made into a documentary, *Inheritance of War.*

When Doug Cervi learned through that newspaper article about the book and the documentary, he contacted me to see how he could get a copy.

"I need something visually to show my students," he explained. "How can I make that happen?"

"I'll send you a book and a DVD tomorrow," I told him over the phone. I also explained about my book *Autodidactic* and my literacy initiative. That led to the invitation to come to Oakcrest High School and speak to the students. It was then that I got to see a master teacher in his element. A man who is everything that's right about teaching.

I asked Doug what he considered the keys to being a good teacher. He didn't hesitate in listing his top two qualities. First and foremost, he said, you have to care about the kids. Second, you need to be passionate about what you're teaching. "When they see and feel that passion, they'll respond," he said.

Doug told me he didn't set out to be a teacher. His first plan was to play football for a living. He was a good player in high school and college. He was team captain his senior year at Widener University in Pennsylvania, where he played right guard on the offensive line. But the NFL has only so many openings, and when professional football didn't come calling, he went to plan B. And it still wasn't teaching.

"I wanted to be a football coach," he explained. "To do that you have to become a certified teacher."

So he got his teaching certificate.

The first job offer he received was from his alma mater. Four years after he graduated, he came back to Oakcrest High School to help coach football, wrestling, and baseball and teach history—for the princely sum of $7,800 a year.

"I told myself, 'If this doesn't work out, I'm out of here,'" remembered Cervi.

But it did work out. He spent forty-one years at Oakcrest (he retired in 2014 and now teaches at Stockton University), transferring his love of history—and sports—to literally thousands of students whom he came to love even more.

He found a valuable parallel between coaching sports on the playing field and teaching history in the classroom. To be successful in both, you need to have an integral relationship with the kids; you have to make sure that you are each chasing the same goal. You're in it together. When one wins, both win; when one loses, both lose.

And no two students are exactly alike.

"My belief is that every kid can learn, but they all learn differently and you've got to figure that out," said Doug.

Something else he discovered as a young teacher was the need to keep the students constantly engaged. "You can't Power Point and lecture for two hours: that will bore them to death. If you're going to do it right you better get good at telling stories. If you can't tell a good story you're done, you're dead in the water."

By his fourth or fifth year, he realized something else: no matter how great his stories were, bringing in guest speakers was going to make them even greater.

That's when he started bringing history to life by introducing his students to the actual history makers. After showing film clips from the popular *Band of Brothers* documentary series, for example, he brought in soldiers who were in the film. When he'd teach about swing music, he'd bring in a musician who played swing music. When the subject was the Great Depression, he'd bring in a banker and show his students genuine silver dollars.

The subject he became most passionate about was the Holocaust. He made it a life goal to learn and document all he could about the tragic episode in which some six million Jews were exterminated by Adolf Hitler and the Nazis during World War II. He personally reached out to any number of Holocaust experts and scholars for more information on the subject. He tracked down a man on the Internet, Rudolf Vrba, who had escaped from Auschwitz and written a book that had been translated into

English. He used material from the book, along with other sources, to shed even more light on life inside the concentration camps and the horrors that occurred there. The state of New Jersey was impressed to the point that it asked Mr. Cervi to help rewrite the curriculum on the Holocaust, a project that took three years.

"The Holocaust became the most important subject that I taught," he said. "If we don't learn as human beings how to treat each other, we're doomed to let history repeat itself."

In my observations of Doug Cervi's classroom and interaction with his students, I saw a tremendous respect between teacher and pupil. Mr. Cervi is the kind of person who keeps a mental record of the kids who don't raise their hands during his class, and then makes a point of reaching out to them after the bell rings to see how they're doing and make sure they're not feeling neglected.

In the museum next to his classroom, alongside mannequins of soldiers in uniforms and display cases filled with World War II memorabilia, he has more than four hundred books. He's read every one of them, he tells the kids. And they should too. He laments the decline of book reading. "Reading is almost a lost art in this country, unfortunately," he said.

I asked Mr. Cervi his views on the state of education in America. His chief complaint was with the frequent state- and federal-mandated testing—in his last year of teaching, no less than twenty-one days out of the one hundred eighty days in a New Jersey school year were taken up by such tests. "I don't understand the focus on testing," he said. "You have the ACT and the SAT, isn't that enough? What makes kids want to learn is the person in front of the classroom. Leave the teachers alone, let them teach."

(Mr. Cervi is not saying that all testing is bad; he's saying that testing for twenty-one days for assessment purposes is of no use. As pointed out by Professor Bjork in chapter 7, low-stakes quizzing and testing not only enhance learning but also reduce anxiety on any subsequent high-stakes tests.)

He said that testing methods for evaluating teachers changed six times during his four-plus decades of teaching, and yet "none of those methods for the most part helped anyone do a better job in the classroom." A better way of grading teachers, he suggested, is to ask the students. "Want to know who the crummy teachers are? Ask the kids. They know who cares about them and who's trying to do a good job."

After forty-one years in the trenches, his view is that "ninety-something percent of teachers really want to change the world; they want to do it right."

On my last night in May's Landing, Doug treated me to dinner at his favorite restaurant, an Italian place called Maplewood.

When our food arrived, I started to eat my spaghetti when I heard this from across the table: "You're cutting your pasta with a knife!"

I looked up to see Cervi looking on in horror as I went at the noodles with my fork and knife. It was as if I were committing homicide.

"I'm Italian!" he exclaimed. "If my mother knew I was eating with somebody who cut noodles with a knife!"

He let the thought hang.

I put down the knife.

He then proceeded to show me how to twirl the pasta into a spoon, the way real Italians do.

I picked up my spoon to try it, idly commenting about the tasty marinara sauce.

"And by the way, it's gravy, not sauce," he said.

Great teachers are never at a loss for a teaching moment. They never stop teaching, never stop sharing what they know with the people they love.

11

The Principal

THE STUDENTS AT WEST Shores High School sit up and pay attention when their principal tells them he knows what they're going through—because they know he's gone through it too.

Richard Pimentel was playing basketball when we first met. I had come to the campus of West Shores High in the California desert to talk to him about my literacy program and my book *Autodidactic*. At the office, I asked to see the principal. An aide gestured toward a scrum of students playing a wild game of basketball on the playground, singling out a young man in a cowboy hat who seemed to be the main object of the kids' enthusiasm and intensity.

"That's him," I was told.

I stood at the edge of the court and waited until the game ended, at which point an exhausted Mr. Pimentel, battered but still standing, came over and warmly shook my hand. Later on, I asked him why he'd kept playing basketball when I'd given him a perfect excuse to exit the pummeling he was taking.

He smiled. "My kids come first," he said. "I make no excuse for that. My kids always come first."

My autodidactic travels have taken me to dozens and dozens of high schools all over the country. I've covered the socioeconomic gamut from rich to poor. I've been to little schools and big schools, private schools and public schools, charter schools and home schools. No administrator has affected me so, or given me more hope for the future of education in America, than the man in charge at West Shores.

West Shores is located in Salton City, California, a place that never gets confused with Beverly Hills. Salton City sits next to the Salton Sea, the largest body of water in California and also, because of its salinity, the most useless. The lake was largely formed when an engineering miscalculation during an unusually wet season in the early 1900s drained a mass of water from the Colorado River into the desert basin, where it has remained and stagnated ever since. A few attempts to turn the shoreline into resort property have been largely unsuccessful, resulting in a rural area that has become primarily a refuge for low-income residents who mostly work as laborers in the nearby fields.

Drawing from a sizeable portion of western Imperial County, West Shores High School has a student body of some five hundred students, grades seven through twelve. Ninety-two percent are Hispanic, with the other eight percent Caucasian, Native American, and African American. Less than half of the kids live in a home with both parents; many are raised by grandparents or other relatives. The poverty level is such that there isn't a kid in the school who doesn't qualify for some form of food assistance. The cafeteria at West Shores doesn't even have a cash register.

English is a second language for many of the students; some have recently arrived from Mexico. They're new, disoriented, and frightened in a strange culture.

Richard Pimentel knows where they are coming from. Quite literally. It wasn't all that long ago that he was one of them.

He understood barely a word of English when he arrived in America in 1990 at the age of fifteen. Ironically, it was pursuit of more education that prompted the move. Richard had just finished ninth grade in Mexico, the last level of public school available in that country to foreigners. The ironic part is that Richard had been born in America—back in 1975 during a time when his father had briefly found work in Escondido, near San Diego, before he and Richard's mother were apprehended by border authorities and deported back to Mexico with their new baby. That made Richard a legitimate U.S. citizen, with all the rights and privileges attached to that distinction, including making him ineligible for a Mexican education past ninth grade. To continue his schooling beyond that, he had to leave Mexico.

His older sister, mother, and father came with him in 1990. They first settled in south-central Los Angeles, where not being able to speak English broke Richard in quickly. The family was living in a gang zone. On one side were the Crips, on the other the Bloods. Both of them beat up Richard because each thought he belonged to the other side, and since he couldn't speak English he couldn't tell them he was just trying to get to the public swimming pool, the first one he'd ever seen.

The Principal

The Pimentels soon relocated to Huntington Beach, where they rented a garage in what is known as the Slater slums. "But it was a two-car, man, it was huge!" is how Richard explained it in his glass-half-full way. "I lived a great, great life. I didn't know I didn't have anything; just being in the country was awesome."

When he enrolled at Fountain Valley High School, officials there weren't any more sure what to do with him than the Crips and the Bloods. Thinking he had learning disabilities because he couldn't speak the language, they first put him in a special education class. But it wasn't long before Pimentel's intelligence and drive rose to the surface. His older sister had enrolled in an adult education class at night to learn English and typing skills. He tagged along with her. Every day during the summer before enrolling and after attending his high school classes, he would spend his nights learning English as well as typing.

By his senior year, Richard was a top student, with the kind of grades that could get him into a good college. His perfect math score on the SAT also didn't hurt.

The problem was, he didn't know he needed to contact the schools he was interested in attending. In Mexico, colleges recruit the students, not the other way around.

It was very late in the application process when a school counselor came to the rescue, asking Richard where he'd sent college applications. "Wait, I have to apply?" was his answer. As fortune had it, an alumnus of Notre Dame happened to be visiting the office that day and suggested he apply there. Richard sent in his application just in time. He didn't have to wait long for a response. Not only did Notre Dame want him, they offered him a full ride—plus tuition, books, fees, and enough of a monthly stipend that enabled him to occasionally fly back home to California to see his family.

Three years since walking across the border from Mexico, unable to speak English, Richard Pimentel was on his way to South Bend, Indiana, for an education at one of America's most prestigious universities.

Four years later, he had his degree in biochemistry.

His next move was equally as unpredictable and unlikely. He decided to join the army. He chose the infantry as his preferred branch and became a combat medic, excelling to the point that he was named Soldier of the Year for the fabled 101st Airborne Division while earning his wings.

Back in California after his army stint was over, he interviewed for a teaching job at Coachella Valley High School simply because he wanted to get in some practice at selling himself in a job interview. His plan was to apply to some of the big pharmaceutical companies and finally put that college degree in biochemistry to good use.

He was still very much in military mode when the school officials who were conducting the interview, suitably impressed by his résumé, asked, "If you for some reason got the job, when would you be able to start?"

"I'd start tomorrow, sir!" said Pimentel.

And the officials said, "OK!"

As Pimentel related this story to me, he explained that, since he unexpectedly got the job, he thought what could it hurt to give it a try. He figured he'd be lucky if he lasted through the day as a teacher.

But after one period, "Oh my gosh, I loved those kids! Within one hour I knew what I wanted to do with my life!"

So that's how a born-in-America Mexican immigrant, Notre Dame graduate, U.S. Army Soldier of the Year became an educator.

Rich taught AP biology and chemistry before moving into the administrative side of things, recognizing his rather unique skill set that allows him to relate so well, and so compassionately, with kids who aren't born into the world on third base, as they say. At West Shores High School, he looks into the eyes of his students and sees himself.

His educational philosophy is simple and straightforward and can be seen clearly in the three sacrosanct rules he insists on for his teachers:

One. They must care for the students they teach. "If you don't love the kids, you're in the wrong place."

Two. They must have a plan for having their students read. "Reading is fundamental to everything else you learn."

Three. They must have a plan for making sure their students interact with what they've read. "Students have to be able to understand and relate to the material. Just reading isn't enough; what you read needs to make sense."

He also has two unspoken rules:

Every student needs to feel an adult touch twice a day—"A pat on the back, shake their hand, whatever." And every student needs to hear their name at least twice a day from an adult. "It's special. And it's free!"

The point is, if you don't first reach them on a personal, human level, you'll never reach them on a math and science and English level.

One of his outside-the-classroom tactics is what he calls his ice cream club. It all started shortly after he came to West Shores and idly asked some students when was the last time they'd gone to an ice cream parlor.

These were the answers he got: "Never." "Two years ago with my dad." "What's an ice cream parlor?"

"So I have my ice cream club," Richard explained. "I take the students on hikes or outings and we talk, and then we go and get ice cream after."

Empathy and understanding notwithstanding, Mr. Pimentel doesn't give his students any free passes, however. Hard times are no excuse for not trying. A man who spent his teenage years living in a two-car garage doesn't countenance anyone feeling sorry for themselves. Playing the victim card doesn't fly at his school.

To make a success out of your life, he contends, "You've got to be OK with what you have. There's nothing wrong with ambition. But there's everything wrong with not being happy with what you've been given. You have to be grateful, no matter what."

A principal at another area high school had told Mr. Pimentel about my literacy program and suggested it might be a good fit for West Shores, which is how I came to make this extraordinary principal's acquaintance.

After I explained my program to him, he embraced it immediately. Someone wanted to encourage his students to read and increase their vocabulary! And every kid would get a free book!

I've never had anyone say "yes" faster.

Standing in front of the students at West Shores was both humbling and inspiring for me. They are a speaker's dream: attentive, inquisitive, receptive. I spoke in both Spanish and English, which I think under the circumstances helped a great deal. And this is no knock on some of the wealthier high schools I've visited, but the kids at West Shores seemed to be especially grateful when at the end of the assembly I handed each of them a copy of *Autodidactic* as they left the auditorium. I'm sure that for many of them it was the first book they'd ever personally owned.

I was flattered when my book was adopted into the school's curriculum and became required reading in West Shore's advisory classes. Among the finest compliments of my life was the backhanded one I received from

Richard Pimentel, when in mock amazement he said to me, "You were the first person who told them not to use poverty as an excuse—'Read, that's your escape,' and they really listened! I've been trying to tell them that the whole time I've been here!"

I thanked him and quoted Mark Twain, "An expert is anybody from out of town."

But there's no question what's making things work at West Shores High. It's a great administrator and the great staff he's assembled. Like all schools, the success rate isn't perfect. West Shores still has more than its fair share of problems. But it has more than its fair share of successes as well. Consider this amazing fact: for two straight years, in 2015 and 2016, West Shores students were awarded a Gates Millennium Scholarship. These scholarships are given by the Bill & Melinda Gates Foundation to high-performing minority students who might not otherwise have the opportunity to go to college. Recipients receive all expenses related to their college education at whatever university they choose for as long as they want to stay in school. One of the West Shores winners is at UCLA, and the other is at the University of California, Davis.

Only a thousand Gates Millennium Scholarships are awarded each year around the country, and West Shores High School was honored with two in back-to-back years.

Jennifer Gopar, the 2015 recipient and daughter of field laborers, wasn't even going to apply for the scholarship because she reasoned it was out of her reach.

Then You Know Who stepped in.

Remembered Mr. Pimentel: "She said to me, 'That's the best scholarship. I don't know.' And I told her, 'You don't have a choice not to apply.'"

Richard Pimentel understands the value of the one. During one of my visits, he shared with me the story from his days as a science teacher. A new student who barely spoke English told him he wanted to be the best runner on the cross-country team.

"I noticed he didn't say 'a good runner,'" said Pimentel. "He said 'best runner.' I mentioned that he could be the best student, the best college student, the best leader. He accepted the challenge and committed to learning the language."

That young man became part of two cross-country championship teams and the school's only track and field championship team in over twenty years. He was salutatorian of his graduating high school class, studied engineering at Cal Poly Pomona, and within three years was named his company's Engineer of the Year.

He wanted to be just like Mr. Pimentel, a migrant living the American dream—and he succeeded.

"We don't know how many lives we touch," said Mr. Pimentel. "But the thought I've at least inspired one honors me beyond words."

The truth is, none of us knows what the ripples will bring from the pebbles we scatter in the water.

12

The President

THE FOUR DAYS I traveled with President Michael T. Benson to Notre Dame in the summer of 2010 left an indelible impression on me. That trip is not to be forgotten. It was a cram course in "Higher Education: Why It Matters, and Why It Must Be Preserved at All Costs."

Of all the doors that opened for me due to writing *Autodidactic*, none came as a more unexpected and pleasant surprise than the four days I spent in the passenger seat holding a university president captive while he was driving his car.

At the beginning of the summer of 2010, for 1,657 miles—all the way from Cedar City, Utah, to the University of Notre Dame campus in South Bend, Indiana—I quizzed Michael T. Benson, while at the wheel of his Infiniti M37, about his thoughts and philosophy on higher education in America. And whenever he would come up for air, I would ask him for more.

If your image of a university president is a person wearing a buttoned-down business suit, stuffy, imperious, unapproachable, cast all that aside. Mike Benson is none of that. His charm and ability to connect with people account for his meteoric rise through the ranks of American higher education.

At the age of thirty-six, he was the youngest college president in the history of the Utah System of Higher Education when he was appointed to lead Snow College in Ephraim, Utah. Five years later, at age forty-one, he became president of Southern Utah University (SUU), a school of ten thousand students in Cedar City, Utah. Seven years after that, still not in his fifties, he moved on to take over as president of Eastern Kentucky University (EKU) in Richmond, Kentucky, with a student body of seventeen thousand.

At each stop, he has made historic marks. At Snow College, he was responsible for brokering a partnership between the rural Utah college and the Juilliard School, the acclaimed New York arts academy. At SUU, the school became Utah's only designated public liberal arts and sciences university, leading to admission into the prestigious Council of Public Liberal Arts Colleges. During his tenure at EKU, the school reached its highest-ever enrollment and graduation rates.

In addition to all that, his fundraising has set new standards. He raised more money during his five years at Snow than the school had raised in its previous 115 years combined. At SUU, he raised $105 million in just seven years. At EKU, private support has likewise reached record levels.

I met President Benson in the fall of 2009, three years into his time at SUU. Always open to trying new things, after hearing about my literacy and learning initiative from a friend of a friend, he reached out to me to be a part of SUU's orientation week for incoming students, called the T-Bird Flight School, that is held each year prior to the start of classes in the fall. I spent two days in Cedar City, talking to fifteen hundred freshmen about literacy and learning and signing copies of *Autodidactic*.

That appearance led to a relationship with SUU that lasted four more years—until Mike left for EKU in 2013. Our views and personalities meshed well, and not long after my initial visit, he appointed me as Special Assistant to the President and Distinguished Fellow for International Engagement.

As the president's envoy, I was able to assist the school in expanding its international outreach. Through my contacts in Africa, we arranged for a visit to the SUU campus by Hassan Jallow, a respected judge from The Gambia whom the United Nations appointed chief prosecutor for the International Criminal Tribunal for Rwanda—the court that prosecuted war crimes committed during the Rwandan civil war. Jallow's visit was followed by that of Abdoulaye Wade, then president of Senegal, the first-ever visit by a sitting president of a country to SUU. In addition to my international work, I was able to arrange for a visit to Cedar City by my UCLA psychologist friend Robert Bjork, who brought his team of cognitive scientists to the university for a seminar.

Michael T. Benson's own academic résumé was hardly lacking. He'd gotten his bachelor's degree from Brigham Young University in political science, with a double minor in history and English, and followed that with a doctorate—in Modern Middle Eastern History—from Oxford University in England. He wrote his PhD dissertation about Harry S. Truman, which led to his authoring a book, *Harry S. Truman and the Founding of*

Israel, which won critical praise as a landmark work on the subjects of U.S. foreign policy and presidential history.

All that notwithstanding, after eight years as a university president, he decided he wanted to go back to school.

He applied (and was accepted) to the Mendoza College of Business at the University of Notre Dame to study for a master's degree in Non-profit Administration.

To understand Mike's enrolling at Notre Dame at age forty-four is to understand a true autodidact. This is a person who spent two years in Italy as a young man, learning to speak fluent Italian. He spent three years in England, studying at Oxford. He visited Israel no less than sixteen times and lived there as a study-abroad student at the BYU Jerusalem Center for Near Eastern Studies and as a visiting graduate student at the Hebrew University of Jerusalem. He will never stop learning. Continuing his education is a really big part of who Mike Benson is.

The idea to drive to Notre Dame was Mike's, so he could have a car for the summer. The plan was to set out for Notre Dame as soon as SUU's graduation ceremonies ended in May. The impetus to bring me along was not so I could sit in the passenger seat and pick his brain about education; it was golf.

Mike is a man of endless energy and countless passions. A genuine Renaissance man. In addition to being a scholar, he is a classical pianist, a sub–three hour marathon runner (2:52 at Boston), and during his undergraduate days, he played on the junior varsity basketball team at BYU. And then there's golf. From the moment he first picked up a club, the game grabbed him. Every time he passes a golf course, he wants to stop the car and play it.

The sights he most wanted to see between Utah and Indiana weren't Pikes Peak, the Black Hills, and the Mississippi River; they were golf courses.

He showed me our itinerary. First, we'd play at Castle Pines Golf Club outside Denver, then Butler National Golf Club in Oak Brook, Illinois, followed by Black Sheep Golf Club in Sugar Grove, Illinois, and, as the crown jewel, the Chicago Golf Club, one of the oldest and most prestigious—and hardest to get on—golf courses in America.

If you think the man who ran the Boston Marathon in under three hours and played college basketball and speaks fluent Italian and is an accomplished concert pianist is going to play golf and not keep score and make a contest out of it, you're nuts. Mike set up a tournament between the two of us. I suggested we call it, in memory of my friend and mentor, the Grant Fitts Memorial. When I told Stuart Fitts we were naming the competition in his father's honor, Stuart volunteered to provide a beautiful crystal trophy for the winner.

I was one stroke ahead after our first three rounds, but Chicago got one of its famous thunderstorms the morning we were to play our final round at the Chicago Golf Club, raining us out. Mike had to be at Notre Dame to start classes, so we had to move on. I immediately called myself the temporary winner and took the trophy home and put it in my den. (Ever since, Mike has insisted that we finish the match. I keep telling him we have to finish it at the Chicago Golf Club, and we haven't made it back there yet.)

Mike's energy amazed me. After playing golf every day, we'd get in the car and he'd drive for nine hours straight, talking the entire time about his love for education. I sat in the passenger seat, the recipient of thirty-six hours of unfettered lecturing on higher education.

He opened my eyes to what a treasure our universities are, the vital role they play, and how important it is to maintain them and protect them from those who want to undermine their importance. It is a great irony to me that in America, it's our educators, especially those who run our universities, who are among the most intelligent, capable, and creative thinkers among us, and yet their views and recommendations often go unheard, or at best "under heard," by policy makers who fund and implement our educational infrastructure.

As the miles rolled on across Colorado, then Kansas, Missouri, Illinois, and finally Indiana, I filed away as much of President Benson's wisdom and philosophy as I could. In our many conversations in the years since (and more than a few more road trips), I have listened as he has taught me even more. Here, in no particular order, are what I consider some of his most important points:

Education Is Freedom

"The more education you have the more free you are in life," Mike told me. "That is the best case for getting as much education as you possibly can."

He quoted a personal hero of his, the inimitable George Washington Carver, who famously said, "Education is the key to unlock the golden door of freedom."

The life of George Washington Carver makes a great case in point. Born a slave in Missouri shortly after the start of the Civil War, he was soon to be liberated by the war's outcome. Desperate for higher education, when he was in his mid-twenties he borrowed three hundred dollars from the bank—no small sum in 1888—so he could go to college. He was the first black student admitted to Iowa State Agricultural College in Ames, Iowa, where he obtained bachelor's and master's degrees in botany and joined the faculty as the school's first black professor. He left Iowa State when he was asked to take over as head of the agriculture department at Tuskegee Institute (now Tuskegee University) in Alabama. He stayed at that post for forty-seven years and became one of the country's first ag-scientists. His pioneering research in the areas of sustainable farming techniques and crop rotation revolutionized how America looked at agriculture. He advocated raising a variety of crops and experimenting in how they could be used. He came up with 105 different uses for peanuts. Three American presidents—Theodore Roosevelt, Calvin Coolidge, and Franklin Roosevelt—used him as an agriculture adviser.

After his death in 1943, a national monument was erected to his memory in Missouri, not far from where he had grown up uneducated and dirt poor. He was featured posthumously on not one but two commemorative postage stamps, one in 1948 and another in 1998; and two U.S. Navy vessels, a cargo ship and a nuclear submarine, have borne his name.

He bequeathed his entire estate, some sixty-thousand dollars (about one million in today's dollars), to establish the George Washington Carver Foundation to help others in search of education and freedom.

Financial freedom, Mike explained, was only part of George Washington Carver's liberation.

"There are studies out there that show how valuable education can be in how much money you can make," he said. "A bachelor's degree will be worth so much more than a high school diploma and so on. That's fine and good; you're going to earn more money. But I'm a big believer that there are benefits far beyond the economic. There are also studies that show the more educated you become, you're going to have better health, you're going to be more religious, you're going to be more involved in your community, you're going to be interested in many more things. Maybe you'll run for office, maybe you'll volunteer more, maybe you'll travel more. The end result is you are going to have a better quality of life. That's the freedom education gives you."

Knowledge Is Power

Mike's unwavering contention is that going to college to study the liberal arts—the so-called humanities subjects of history, sociology, economics, psychology, philosophy, literature, art, religion, and so forth—is the very best way to equip yourself with the tools that allow you to understand and appreciate the world and get along with its inhabitants.

"Some maintain that 'liberal arts' majors result in less-than-ideal job prospects," President Benson once wrote in a newspaper editorial expressing this viewpoint. "Indeed, recently one presidential candidate called for 'more welders, less philosophers' while a well-known venture capitalist quipped that English graduates 'end up working in a shoe store.' Sadly, this sentiment seems to be growing.

"And yet, liberal arts majors represent the undergraduate courses of study, respectively, of Jamie Dimon, CEO of JP Morgan Chase; Ronald Reagan, fortieth president of the United States; Samuel Palmisano, former CEO of IBM; Condoleezza Rice, former secretary of state; John Watson, CEO of Chevron; and Carl Icahn, billionaire Wall Street mogul. And let's not forget J. K. Rowling of Harry Potter fame. She completed a bachelor's in French and Classics."

Mike is quick to note that not every art history major will run a Fortune 500 company or write blockbuster fiction, but the success stories he cites—and he could name countless others—illustrate the value of going to school to learn rather than going to school to specialize.

He points to studies that show that employers are interested not only in people who have the requisite skills to be a computer programmer, say, or a chemical engineer, but in those who are well traveled, who can speak another language, who understand human nature, who have a reputation for doing well in social settings.

"What employers want hasn't changed," he says. "In every new hire, the number one attribute is the ability to work well in a group. Two is the ability to communicate. Three is the ability to think rationally. Four is to have empathy. Five is to be able to read critically. All five are the top things that are developed in a traditional liberal arts training."

The Latin word *libero* is the root of "liberal," Mike points out. "*Libero* means to make free, to open one's mind to a broad spectrum of opinions and philosophies." That is precisely what a liberal arts education does.

If he had it to over again, Mike told me, "I'd be an English literature major. Where else are you going to be able to read all those great books?"

Education Widens Horizons

One of the great benefits of our colleges and universities, Mike stresses, is the forum they provide for a healthy exchange of viewpoints. Being exposed to the philosophies, opinions, and points of view of others, while also being able to express our own, is at the heart of education and learning, and has been at least since Socrates and Aristotle and Plato debated in Athens. It is how we expand our horizons and open our eyes and ears to other possibilities and ways of doing things.

He is no fan of restricting anyone from expressing their point of view, "no matter how anathema it might be to how we feel."

"Our job is not to shelter anyone from ideas, but create an environment where those ideas can be shared openly and freely, without restriction or recrimination," he maintains. "If we can't have a free exchange of ideas on a college campus, where else are we going to have it?"

Higher Education Is a Cornerstone of Democracy

America's institutions of higher learning aren't just the result of a free society, they play a major role in making sure it endures and thrives.

Several years after our road trip, Mike, in conjunction with his colleague and coauthor Hal Boyd, wrote "College for the Commonwealth," which puts forth a masterful defense of the university as an important pillar of American democracy. They spell out the case that the inertia that comes from a highly educated populace greatly preserves America's ideals, principles, and standard of living. With knowledge comes protection from decay and dissent.

The book praises two momentous social policies "that changed forever American higher education," paving the way for increased access to higher education. The first was the 1862 Morrill Land-Grant Act. The second was the 1944 G.I. Bill.

Justin S. Morrill was a senator from Vermont who, as a young man, had received little education beyond the rudimentary basics, a normal enough situation at the time for anyone in America who was not wealthy or a member of the upper class. America's few universities, like Harvard and Yale, were reserved for the elite.

But Justin Morrill was a self-learner—a true autodidact who devoured books—and the more he educated himself throughout his life the more he lamented not having had the advantage of the kind of advanced schooling available to only a few. As hard as he tried, he knew he could never catch up. But he could help others. In the U.S. Senate, he introduced his "college bill" designed to make higher education available to the masses. "We have schools to teach the art of manslaying and make masters of 'deep-throated engines' of war," he said, "and shall we not have schools to teach men the way to feed, clothe, and enlighten the great brotherhood of man?"

President Abraham Lincoln signed Morrill's bill into law in the opening months of the Civil War. The bill apportioned land to each state in the union to "support at least one college" that would provide "liberal and practical education and focus mainly on agricultural and mechanical arts, as well as military instruction."

A century and a half later, 106 thriving land-grant universities—stretching from Texas A&M to Cornell to Penn State to Michigan State to the University of Tennessee to MIT to Oregon State and all that lie in between—testify to Morrill's vision.

As Boyd and Benson point out in their book: "Today, the original land-grant universities have graduated countless civil servants, business leaders, and luminaries in the arts and sciences. Alumni include more than five hundred Rhodes Scholars, five hundred federal legislators, two hundred governors, and a handful of U.S. Supreme Court justices, vice presidents, and foreign heads of state. Over the years, hundreds of Pulitzer Prize winners and Nobel laureates have affiliated with these institutions as students, professors, and researchers. Currently, the CEOs of Apple, Walmart, Ford, Verizon, BP, Berkshire Hathaway, McKesson, and Koch Industries—eight of the globe's largest companies—are land-grant alumni. The aggregate endowments of the schools total more than $64 billion, and by a conservative estimate, they annually educate more than 1.5 million students. In short, these institutions significantly impact the nation and the everyday lives and careers of Americans."

Equally significant was the Servicemen's Readjustment Act of 1944—commonly known as the G.I. Bill— that the U.S. Congress passed toward the end of World War II.

Promoted by the American Legion to aid service members returning from the war, the bill sailed through both houses. Expectations were low in projecting how many G.I.s would actually take advantage of the breaks in tuition and other college fees, but almost immediately the returning veterans began signing up for classes. As Benson and Boyd point out, "By the expiration of the first bill in 1956, nearly half of the sixteen million World War II veterans received one kind of educational training through the program. In 1947 alone, G.I.s accounted for nearly half of all students enrolled in American colleges."

The legacy of learning that was started by those millions of veterans has been handed down to their sons and daughters and their sons and daughters, resulting in a nation where "going to college" has become a common goal for all.

Mike Benson describes our colleges and universities as "sanctuaries of citizenship where young and old come to expand their skills, broaden their horizons, and prepare themselves for the rigors of twenty-first–century citizenship."

The Envy of the World

Sometimes, if we're not careful and dwell too much on the negative, we can lose sight of an American system of higher education that is the world's gold standard. No other country can boast of colleges and universities that educate so many, and do it so well.

Mike likes to quote from a speech by Chase Peterson, a former president of the University of Utah.

"Chase talked about America having many deficits, a trade deficit here, maybe a moral deficit there," says Mike. "But he said there's one area where we don't have any kind of a deficit, and that's higher education. And he was right. People come from all over the world to study at our universities. We have the greatest system the world has ever known."

The President

The *Times of London,* he notes, annually publishes a list of the world's top universities. Every year, seventeen or eighteen of the top twenty-five are in the United States.

"We are, and we remain, the envy of the entire world."

The four days I traveled with President Michael T. Benson to Notre Dame in the summer of 2010 left an indelible impression on me. That trip is not to be forgotten. It was a cram course in higher education: why it matters, and why it must be preserved at all costs.

13

The Politician

INITIALLY, WHEN I LAUNCHED my literacy and learning program nationwide, my grand plan was to reach every student in America. There was nothing small, nothing modest, nothing self-effacing about what I wanted to accomplish. I would have every student in the country not only reading a book, but understanding what they were reading, and enjoying it! No small goal.

If that sounds grandiose, bear in mind, I had just left a world where megalomania was normal. The trial bar is not known for its humility. It's not enough if you win your verdict; it's how big the verdict is. It's not "Do you have a Rolex watch?" It's "How many Rolexes do you have?" As a trial lawyer, I spent thirty-plus years in a profession where grandiosity is an everyday thing. That's the environment I came out of, and that worldview was blinding my view of reality in the world of education.

It was only natural that I thought I could start a revolution. My program was successful, and I was seeing how I was changing lives. If I could affect one student and one school at a time, then why not share it with the entire country? I thought about building a web page and starting a blog. I thought about filming the talk and posting the video online. There was no end of my ideas to make my program national. But to foment a revolution, I knew I needed friends in high places. I needed the power that alliances make. I could not do it by myself.

To that end, I arranged, through my brother Rick, for a sit-down lunch meeting with Gary Herbert. Herbert is the governor of Utah, a state where my ties are many. I spent my college years in Utah. My family's roots are there. It was a good place to start.

The governor graciously heard me out as I laid out my hopes and goals of integrating my initiative into the state education system. Together we would spread the principles of autodidacticism. That was my pitch.

Every student would see the light, start reading, and take charge of their own education. We would put a new face on education.

The governor's reaction was slightly more subdued. After hearing me describe my plan, Governor Herbert complimented me on what I was trying to do and then informed me that he had two great committees working on similar goals and that he would let them know about my ideas.

I had a similar encounter with Dr. Raul Ruiz. Dr. Ruiz was in the midst of a campaign running for the U.S. Congress from my district in California—a seat he would eventually win. He had enlisted my support in his race, and I took the opportunity to enlist his support for my program. I couldn't have found a more receptive listening ear. Raul is the personification of an autodidact. Born in Mexico, raised in America by farmworkers, he graduated with honors from UCLA and went on to obtain his medical degree from Harvard. In addition, he received two more graduate degrees from Harvard, a Master of Public Policy from the Kennedy School of Government, and a Master of Public Health from the Harvard School of Public Health. No one had to tell Dr. Raul Ruiz about the value and importance of education.

His response was the same as Governor Herbert's. He expressed great enthusiasm for my project and told me that once he got to Washington he wanted me to help him form a committee that would explore ways to make my initiative part of the federal education system.

After meeting with both politicians, I realized I was a stranger in their world, and they were strangers in mine. They were policy makers, their goals and objectives weren't my goals and objectives. What they were facing wasn't what I was facing. They each had an entire system to manage; I had one initiative. They were looking at a much bigger mosaic with myriad stakeholders and countless interest groups. All I wanted to do was tell a kid to pick up a book and read it—just the sort of idea that dies quickly in a committee.

The politicians opened my eyes to the complexity of public education. I began to realize why it is that even billionaires the likes of Michael Bloomberg and Bill Gates haven't been able to move the needle very far, despite all their money and their efforts. Public education is too big, too overwhelming, for quick fixes or one-size-fits-all solutions.

This realization allowed me to step back and identify where I could fit in, what I wanted my niche to be. I understood I couldn't scale my initiative to mesh with the bureaucracy and reach the multitudes; that just wasn't feasible. It is a one-on-one program. The personal touch from me to the student—and the student to me—is absolutely necessary for my message to be heard, and that's not something that translates well to mass production. It really is my one-man crusade. To be successful, it needs to stay simple and unencumbered, as far from politics as possible.

But meeting with politicians was invaluable for me to see education from a much broader perspective, and especially to recognize in much clearer terms the critical role our elected leaders have as policy makers. The importance of having the right people oversee public education, who keep a steady eye on the future and prepare for the inevitable changes, cannot be overstated.

We desperately need proactive politicians on education's side—politicians like Greg Hughes.

I met Greg through my son Brett. Greg was Speaker of the House of Representatives in Utah. After hearing from Brett about my autodidactic assembly, he invited me to speak at his daughter's school: Corner Canyon High School in Draper, Utah.

That speech and the relationship that developed led to many conversations that helped me understand why Hughes is such a champion of education.

Greg grew up in Pittsburgh, raised by a single mom in tough circumstances. He learned to fight at an early age. To this day, his preferred aerobic workout is a few rounds in the boxing ring. It is no surprise that as a student, lacking incentive and supervision, Hughes was lackadaisical at best. "I was never good at school. My GPA was embarrassing," he told me. "I hated school. I felt like it was jail."

What saved him was a mother who papered his home with books. He might not have studied algebra or biology or history as he should have, but he read at home. He read a lot. By the time he was college age and more serious about getting his education, it was literacy that pulled him through.

That background helps explain not just his support for my literacy program, but the passion and dogged determination that went into the education bill Greg sponsored and passed, against long odds, during the 2014 session of the Utah Legislature.

The bill, officially House Bill 96, the Utah School Readiness Initiative, provides a way to help at-risk kids in their preschool years—ages three through five—get the proper instruction and tutoring so they will be reading at grade level by third grade.

Greg Hughes explained to me what his bill was designed to accomplish. What follows is the "Cliff Notes" summary of his explanation.

Study after study shows that once a child reaches third grade, reading proficiency—knowing your colors, your numbers, your letters, your sounds—is critical to keeping up with the curriculum. Up until third grade you're learning to read, after that you're reading to learn. If you're not at grade level, you will be struggling and behind the curve until you catch on.

"Odds show that if a child is not grade proficient by third grade, they'll be in special education the rest of the time they're in public schools," Greg points out. "As a policy maker that should tell us something: we need to make sure children entering our schools are ready; we need to pull out all the stops to get them ready."

Kids who live in poor conditions are at a decided disadvantage in the race to third grade, with parents who either are not there or, if they are there, are so busy working and trying to make ends meet they don't have the time or resources to give their kids a running start. Someone needs to step in and help fill the gap. Hughes's bill fills the gap.

Here's how the Utah School Readiness Initiative works: a three-, four-, or five-year-old child who would otherwise not be able to pay for a certified preschool—and who qualifies for the program after a series of professional assessments—has his or her tuition covered by funds set aside for the program. The money comes from a mixture of state tax dollars earmarked for education and from investments to the program from private citizens who are supportive of improving education in the state. These investors—typically philanthropists who can afford the risk and want to help disadvantaged youth—are promised a modest return on their money, paid by the state, if the child they sponsor is grade proficient in third grade.

The incentive for the state to fund the program is simple: it will cost much less to educate the child in the long run because it will save the additional dollars required for kids who are not ready for elementary school and have to go through some sort of special education to try and catch up.

Hughes cites studies that show that it costs as much as $30,000 extra for each student who is unprepared when entering kindergarten. By that calculus, paying $4,000 for an at-risk child to attend preschool saves $26,000. That's preventive maintenance at its finest.

In the best-case scenario, the preschool does its job, the investor makes a return on his or her money, the state (by extension the taxpayer) saves money, and the child by third grade is ready to be educated to the fullest.

"Wayne Gretzky said good hockey players have an innate ability to skate toward the puck. The great ones go to where the puck is going to be," Greg said to me in explaining his proactive approach. "If we're going to be good policy makers, if we're going to make a difference down the road, we need to think in terms of where we're going to be five, ten, fifteen years from now. We need to pay more attention to young people before they get to kindergarten. The race to third grade is real."

His School Readiness Bill, he stresses, does not focus resources on children who are fortunate to be in a home effectively teaching literacy or who are economically able to attend existing daycare; it identifies kids at risk and levels the playing field for them.

"We ruffled a lot of feathers with that bill," he says, reflecting on the numerous and contentious legislative debates it took to get HB96 passed. "I had people saying I was a lackey for President Obama [Hughes is a Republican]. You had Democrats hating it, Republicans hating it. When you've got both sides fighting maybe you've got a good plan."

It is Hughes's strong belief that education is managed best at the state level. America is a vast country, with a wide variety of cultures that do not all look at education the same way. That makes administering from a federal perspective difficult at best—as programs such as "No Child Left Behind" have ably demonstrated.

"A school in San Juan County, Utah, doesn't have the same issues as a school on Long Island, New York," Hughes points out. "If you try to apply the same standards to each state it just doesn't work. You find that some states habitually fall below the bar set by the federal government. That's not healthy. Parents don't want to hear that their kids are underperforming; principals don't want to hear it. There's a social stigma attached to that. It can be and usually is counterproductive."

If the point of standards is to motivate students, let the standards be set locally. That said, it's Hughes's view that the executive branch needs to take the lead in establishing an effective game plan for the state. The governor's office is key to setting up a system that meets both current and future educational needs. That may sound strange, coming from a legislator, but Hughes points out that in many states, including Utah, the legislature is in session for only part of the year—a mere forty-five days in Utah—and it takes a full-time hand on the rudder to steer the ship. "What's done from the governor's office can change the trajectory of education and give us a better outcome," he says. "The executive branch should be fully focused on education, and then work with the legislature to make sure the grand plan is implemented."

If he were governor (and he might be one day), Hughes's grand plan would start with identifying and empowering the very people who make education work: educators.

"There are individuals in every state who move the needle in miraculous ways," he says. "I would identify those people and make them ambassadors. Have them talk peer to peer. Show what worked for them and why it worked. What you need are leaders with energy, passion, and creativity, and follow their lead."

If the direction is coming from within, there will be buy in.

"I would have these best and brightest come into challenging schools that have not had success and let them convert their peers on the efforts and strategy they have employed elsewhere. Create turnaround teams that make a difference. Let the educators, the real pros, do it."

Hughes cautions that too much top-down direction can hinder more than it helps. "You can overwhelm your public education system by having too many legislators and governors trying to implement pet programs and systems," he says.

He cites the example of Geoffrey Canada's work in Harlem, where thousands of disadvantaged black children have graduated from college because of the early intervention programs Canada began implementing in the early 2000s. Canada and his "Harlem Children's Zone" attracted attention from all parts of the country; he was the subject of a feature film and a *60 Minutes* segment. The Obama administration was sufficiently impressed that in 2009 it attempted to replicate Canada's system in twenty cities across America. But none of the duplicates succeeded like the original.

"They tried to put it in pill form," says Hughes. "But it doesn't work that way. It's not as easy as laying it out on paper. You cannot just parachute in a program. You can't just throw money at a problem. You need passionate leaders to make it work."

The reason my literacy program intrigued Hughes, he told me, was because he could see it as an effective tool that can work within the system without having to become part of it. He'd like to see every student in America read *Autodidactic: Self-Taught.*

"The reason it resonates so strongly with me is because I see it empowering the student to face everything that life is going to put in front of him. That's what I love about *Autodidactic,*" he said. "I do believe the formula is as simple as to be well-read; to be able to articulate how you feel. That will create an atmosphere where good grades and scholastic achievement will be the natural outcome. Start reading, start writing, and expand your vocabulary—do those three things and I believe it will trigger everything a child needs to learn how to learn."

Education thrives with politicians like Greg Hughes, leaders with vision who cut through the bureaucracy and size up the landscape with rationality and with common sense. "Keep it simple," he says. "Don't play chess in politics. It's really checkers. There is strategy in checkers. I played it with Grandma every day. I'm telling you right now, people overcomplicate public policy all the time. Especially when it comes to education. What we need to focus on is what we are doing with kids. That's what it is all about. We are in a dead heat race to third grade. We want every kid to win that race."

14

His Highness

I USED TO THINK the best way to cross an ocean in an airplane was with a good book. But now I've changed my mind. The best way to cross an ocean is with a good book, flying business class, on Emirates Airlines.

I boarded the flight in Los Angeles and deplaned in Dubai—as rested and relaxed as one could possibly hope for after sixteen hours in the air. The seats were comfortable, the legroom generous, the food Zagat quality, the service outstanding. I opened a copy of John Grisham's newest novel, *The Reckoning,* and lost myself in some indulgent pleasure reading as the polar ice pack passed 38,000 feet below me and the pilot turned south in the direction of the Arabian peninsula.

The sun had long since dipped into the Persian Gulf when we landed, and I was met by a car and driver for the half-hour drive to Sharjah, where accommodations in a five-star hotel awaited. For the next six days I would be treated like a visiting potentate, my hosts anticipating my every need, attending to my every care.

And that, I would discover, was the least of what they could offer me.

I had come halfway around the world to attend the Sharjah International Book Fair, an event hosted yearly in Sharjah city, the capital of the emirate of Sharjah in the federation of the United Arab Emirates (UAE). Of the seven emirates, or states, that make up the UAE, Abu Dhabi and Dubai are the wealthiest and, therefore, best known in the West. Then comes Sharjah, the emirate that borders Dubai on the north.

The invitation had come several weeks earlier. The Sharjah Book Authority officially requested my attendance as a guest lecturer, one of hundreds, at the fair, to talk about literacy and self-education. My *Autodidactic* presentation was going international!

As well read as I thought I was, I must confess I knew next to nothing about Sharjah and less than that about the man who was sponsoring the book fair, His Highness Dr. Sheikh Sultan bin Muhammad Al-Qasimi.

At first glance, I wasn't even sure I'd left home. When I saw Sharjah in the daylight, I thought for a moment I might still be back in Indio. In one direction, beyond the city limits, was a familiar desert landscape, with mountains much like those that stand sentinel at the southeastern border of the Coachella Valley. But on closer look, I saw in the brown and treeless expanse, camels and donkeys making their way across the countryside. That didn't look like California.

In the other direction, I saw cranes. Not the bird variety, but construction cranes, hundreds of them, maybe thousands, seemingly stretching along the Persian Gulf all the way to Dubai. Everywhere I looked, gleaming skyscrapers—office towers, hotels, apartment buildings—dotted the horizon. Luxury resorts hugged the waters of the gulf. The city of Sharjah is a shimmering example of what money, architecture, and planning can accomplish.

The building boom in Sharjah, and throughout the UAE, I learned, can be attributed to two factors: oil and tourism. Oil reserves are most prominent in Abu Dhabi, but all the emirates produce oil, allowing them to build an infrastructure that attracts visitors who come to enjoy luxury accommodations and pleasant weather in the fall and winter.

This is new money, of course, about as new as money gets in the modern world. It's been less than sixty years since the seven emirates (an emirate is a kingdom ruled by a Muslim commander called an emir) that make up the modern UAE began to produce oil. Before that, they were populated largely by wandering tribes of Bedouins tending their flocks. And it's been less than fifty years since the seven kingdoms banded together to create the UAE in December 1971.

A month after that, the kingdom/emirate of Sharjah found itself ruled by His Highness Dr. Sheikh Sultan bin Muhammad Al-Qasimi.

Sharjah was now in the hands of an educator.

His Highness Sheikh Sultan loves learning. He showed that by continuing his own education even after becoming emir. Hardly content with only his bachelor's degree, while taking on the responsibility of ruling Sharjah he also went on to get two doctorates, one in history at Exeter University in England, and another in political geography at Durham University in England. And after that, he taught as a visiting professor at Exeter University and Cairo University.

That is what he did for his own education. But it was what he did for the education of his country that made people stand up and take notice.

The foundation of success for a country and its people is grounded in being literate and learned, the sheikh taught. That is bedrock. A society that is educated is a society that is content and prosperous and self-reliant.

One of his first programs as emir was to create home libraries, distributing books directly to people's homes. Some 45,000 of these libraries were established throughout Sharjah. Sheikh Sultan did precisely what those who study education know is the most critical component of learning: get words in front of children, the earlier the better.

In 1982, ten years into his reign, he started the Sharjah International Book Fair. It was a small gathering at first, but every year, as more and more publishers, authors, teachers, and book lovers flocked to the event, its reach and reputation grew.

By the time I arrived for the thirty-seventh gathering in November 2018, Sharjah's ranked as the third-largest book fair in the world, attracting some 1,874 publishers from seventy-seven countries, featuring 1.6 million individual titles, and attended by 2.23 million visitors. Mingled in, around, and through the eleven days of all things book were no less than 1,800 scheduled events involving 472 presenters, one of whom was me.

On my first day at the fair, I attended the opening ceremonies, a lavish affair held in a smaller hall that sat inside an enormous hall the size of at least a dozen football fields and two stories high. For the next eleven days, this great hall would be filled with booths, exhibitors, presentations, and more books than you could count. The scene was almost not to be believed: actual books being held by actual people, in their hands! In the age of the Internet, no less!

Surrounded by security, the sheikh rose to speak to open the fair. He welcomed the invited dignitaries and guests from around the world. He spoke in Arabic, but earphones were provided for anyone requiring an English translation. (Arabic is Sharjah's official language, but English is the default language and is widely spoken.)

In his remarks, Sheikh Sultan talked about the research he did for the many books he had personally written. He emphasized the need for accuracy and getting the facts right. That caught my attention. Not only was the emir a stickler for truth and attention to detail, but while running the country he had also written several books!

"Those of us who enjoy reading in the emirate of Sharjah are very keen to create a reading community and promote the benefits of reading among children," the emir said to the gathering. "For that reason we provide the best, most suitable books for all the family. We believe that books must be available to all and from this concept we turn book fairs into an oasis of knowledge and enlightenment."

After that, he cut the ribbon to open the fair.

I stood up and applauded. I'd been sitting at a table with three men from Africa, two representing publishing companies in Nigeria, the other in charge of Kenya's state-run publishing arm. I shook hands with them and moved to the front of the hall, where the sheikh was standing, gazing out at the crowd as it dispersed.

I wanted to thank His Highness for inviting me.

I could see this wasn't going to be easy. His Highness was surrounded front, back, and sideways by his security detail. But as we milled about, I began chatting with some of the guards, asking how their day was going, about their families, about their beautiful country. My hope was that they might sense that this strange man from America was harmless enough. I then asked, motioning in the direction of the emir, "Would it be okay if I just said thank you?"

The guards looked at me quizzically. I don't think they often get such a request. They looked me up and down. These were enormous men, obviously well equipped for their roles. They knew that I'd been screened, like everyone else, before entering the room. Standing no more than a foot from the emir, they parted just enough to let me through.

I introduced myself to Sheikh Sultan and said, "I've come a long distance, all the way from California, and I wanted to personally thank you for having me and also for sharing my passion for literacy."

In perfect English, he answered collegially, "Thank *you* for coming. We will change lives."

Pressing my luck, I turned to one of the guards, handed him my phone, and asked the emir, "Can I have my picture taken with you?"

Without missing a beat, he moved toward me for the photo. Pressing my luck again, I asked, "Would it be okay if I put my arm around you?"

This time I'd gone too far.

The sheikh smiled. "Mr. Parkinson, we don't do that here, but I'd be more than honored to hold your hand."

As we shook hands, the guard clicked the photo that is now hanging in a prominent spot in my den in Indio.

With that, I prepared for my first presentation. I was the opening act in what they call "A Tale of Letters," featuring a succession of presenters talking about a variety of topics aligned with books and learning.

A group of high school students had been bussed in for the fair. They filed in and filled the seats in an auditorium in the great hall. There were hundreds of them, all dressed up for the occasion, the boys in ties and the girls in dresses. I found them to be incredibly responsive, inquisitive, and, most of all, gracious. I told them I'd flown from my home in America to their country on my birthday. "Don't feel sorry for me," I said, "but I turned sixty-nine with no one to sing Happy Birthday' to me." At that, they stood up right there on the spot and sang "Happy Birthday."

Afterward, for more than forty-five minutes, every single student stood in line to get my autograph and ask more questions.

The next morning, a black Lexus 460 pulled up in front of the hotel, and I got in the back seat. I was off to my next speech. My driver knew precisely where to go and when to get there. All week it would be like this; everything ran like a Swiss train. The level of service was stunning. I'd walk into the hotel, and it was, "Hello, Mr. Parkinson, is there anything that you need?" "Is there anything you'd like us to do for you?" "What time would you like your car?"

We stopped for a quick bite at McDonald's. It was definitely the nicest McDonald's I'd ever been in. (And by the way, you can't get my usual, a sausage and egg McMuffin, in a Muslim country, but you can get a chicken and egg McMuffin.) I stood in line in front of a man from Belgium and behind a man from Lithuania. That's the nature of the country. Expats are everywhere.

I spoke at high schools in Sharjah, Dubai, and Abu Dhabi, delivering the same message I'd delivered in Mississippi and California and Utah and other places in the United States: literacy and learning are the keys to your happiness and your well-being. Take personal responsibility for your own education. Learn to love books and you will have lifelong companions who will never leave your side and will take you to unimagined places.

In visiting with and observing the students, I sensed that the challenges and issues they face are not so very different from those faced half a world away in America. Bullying, anxiety and stress, a lack of motivation—all are as prevalent in the East as the West. Cheating, the teachers told me, is widespread. That too is a universal concern that knows no borders.

But the positives I saw and felt far outweighed the negatives. The emphasis the country places on education was obvious, carrying with it an energy and an enthusiasm that was almost palpable.

The morning after my third speech, I sat down in the hotel coffee shop and opened a copy of the *Khaleej Times* only to see myself staring back at me. Under the headline "Read More to Succeed in Life, says Author," they had a picture of me with the caption "Celebrated author and literary advocate James Parkinson." I was a book-fair celebrity. The article did a nice job of encapsulating my message.

In the week I was there, I met and talked with the head of the book festival and with numerous heads of publishing companies, writers, booksellers, and book lovers. I was very interested in what they were doing, and they were very interested in what I was doing. It was as if I had died and gone to heaven.

Sheik Sultan's influence on the mindset of the area was undeniable. His favorite saying, "Build minds, not buildings," resonated. Here we were, in the middle of the Arab world, surrounded by unrest, two hours by fast boat from Iran, around the corner from the Yemeni civil war, not far removed from Afghanistan where the Taliban holds sway and Iraq and Syria where ISIS makes life difficult, to say the least, and the conversation wasn't about politics, or war, or oil, or religion. It was about books.

It was clear this was no fad, no passing fancy, this emphasis on education. Since the very beginning of his reign, Sheikh Sultan has made his intention to change the culture clear: he wants everyone to read, and he wants them to read often. Not just some, not just a few, not just the ruling elite. Everyone.

As I looked at the sheikh and listened to him speak, I knew I had found a kindred spirit. Here's a man who has power, wealth, and influence, and he says, in effect, "Guess what? I'm going to use it to help everyone around me." In the little corner of the world where he's in charge, in a tiny country the size of Los Angeles County, with 1.4 million people, he's building an infrastructure founded on education.

It's exactly what I would be doing and saying if I had his money and his power and his time. He's doing wholesale what I'm doing retail!

Equally impressed by the sheikh's efforts was my friend from Mississippi, Wil Colom, who along with Abdul Kinana joined me for part of the festival. Besides his business and philanthropic interests in Tanzania, Wil is heavily involved with the National Association for the Advancement of Colored People (NAACP) in the United States, where he serves as special counsel to NAACP president Derrick Johnson. A major initiative of the NAACP is to find ways to improve the education of young children of color, many of whom fall behind very early in the process of building a foundation of literacy and learning and never seem to catch up.

Wil showed me a letter he sent to the NAACP leadership, proposing changes that fall right in line with Sheikh Sultan's vision. He wrote:

> I believe we are ignoring the level with the greatest potential to influence the achievement of children, and that is their parents. For we know that children across family incomes are far more successful when their parents define education as the first priority, establish learning expectations, and recognize and find supports when a child falls behind. Therefore, I recommend we lead a multi-year campaign that substantially changes the attitude about learning and education within low-performing families and communities. Knowledgeable, engaged parents supporting and advocating for their children—this is the secret sauce of education, that's not so secret. We must say this to our parents and help them make it happen.

Change the culture, in other words. That's what Wil Colom is saying. Change the culture to make education the first priority—just as it is in Sharjah.

On a fine, clear early November morning I bid adieu to Sharjah, just as the *adhan* call went out for morning prayers. The ubiquitous car and driver were at the ready as I walked out of the hotel. The staff wished me safe travels. At the airport in Dubai, I boarded an Emirates Airlines Airbus A380 and settled into my business-class seat. As we flew across the Persian Gulf, I opened my newest book: *My Early Years,* by His Highness Dr. Sultan bin Muhammad Al-Qasimi.

The book is an autobiography of the sheikh's growing-up years. It is one of the many he has written. I learned of a young boy born into a royal family that traces its roots back to the Prophet Muhammed.

But while the history of the Al-Qasimi dynasty includes a chain of sheikhs and emirs as long as your arm—Sheikh Sultan is the eighteenth in a chain of Al-Qasimi rulers in Sharjah that dates back to 1600—it is also a history of constant upheaval and conflict. When Sultan was a child, his father was in exile in Bahrain, unable to live in the land of his inheritance because of internecine infighting. Sultan didn't attend school at all until he was nine years old, and then in a makeshift rural school with palm fronds for a roof. In the 1940s and 1950s, Sharjah was a poor country, and circumstances were difficult. But the young boy was befriended by family and friends who introduced him to books. And that made all the difference.

The pursuit of learning is his life. Recognizing his tremendous commitment to education, universities in no less than fourteen countries—Pakistan, Sudan, Russia, Malaysia, Canada, Armenia, Germany, Jordan, Egypt, Japan, South Korea, France, India, and the United Kingdom—have awarded Sheikh Sultan a total of eighteen honorary doctorates.

"Books will always be the best tool for cross-cultural exchange," the sheikh wisely wrote. "Books focus on our relationship with others and help us look into the variety of values, beliefs, ambitions, and dreams that people can possibly hold. In view of the rapid penetration of technology and communications tools, we need to preserve and promote the values of tolerance, love, and humanity, which books and cultural exchange can do beautifully."

The man is an autodidact! I realized that even more fully when I finished his book. All his life, he has taken responsibility for his own learning—and not only that, but for the learning of all his compatriots. The quintessential autodidact, living out his dream. And mine.

15

The Parents

WHEN WILBUR AND DOROTHY Colom's twins were six years old, Andrew loved to read and constantly had his nose in a book. Scott, on the other hand, expressed no such enthusiasm. He could read, but he'd rather not.

Knowing how much Scott loved sports, one day at the breakfast table his father had a proposition for him.

"I'd like you to read the sports page for me," Wilbur said.

He went on to explain that he was so busy with his law practice that he didn't get to read the sports news like he wanted. He wanted to keep up on all the latest developments, but he just didn't have the time. Would Scott read the newspaper every morning and have a sports report ready when his dad came home from work?

Scott agreed, and Wilbur told me, "That was the last time I heard, 'I don't like to read' from my son."

Of all the components that generate a love of learning, none is as important as parenting. The deft touch of a caring parent is worth more than all the programs, policies, and scholarships combined.

The Coloms told me about another strategy they used to make education something to look forward to and enjoy. Once the twins were seven, Wilbur would take them on a road trip every summer. The deal was that Andrew and Scott could choose the activities they would do each day, but only after they gave their father two hours of what he wanted to do.

Wilbur would take the boys to historic sites and talk to them about history and important events that happened where they were traveling. Sometimes they'd read Shakespeare. After the two hours were up, the boys were in charge.

Scott Colom went on to graduate in English and history from Millsaps College and earn his law degree from the University of Wisconsin. In 2015, he was elected district attorney in Columbus, Mississippi—at age thirty-two, the youngest elected district attorney in America. Andrew Colom graduated in literature and creative writing from Columbia University in New York City and followed that with a master's degree, paid for by a full scholarship from the *New York Times*. He lives in Detroit, where he is a partner in a company that is developing sustainable residential housing.

Certainly, the Colom twins are where they are because of their own initiative and hard work, but there can be no denying the major role played by the emphasis on education they received from their parents.

My friend Wilbur Colom is a great example to me of a person who, no matter how good or how bad the circumstances, turns them into positives. We met through the law. We were both members in good standing of the Republican Trial Lawyers Caucus of the American Trial Lawyers Association (now called the American Association for Justice) when I became president of the organization and Wilbur became president-elect. Thus, it was that a white man from California and a black man from Mississippi became colleagues and, as it would turn out, as close as brothers.

Wil Colom was born and raised in the northern Mississippi town of Ripley in the 1950s. No matter what measurement you're using, for an African American kid in the Deep South in the 1950s, his growing-up years were by no means privileged. He was six years old when Rosa Parks refused to give up her seat in the front of the bus in Montgomery, Alabama, and a new preacher in Montgomery, Martin Luther King, Jr., organized a bus boycott that effectively ignited the civil rights movement. One state removed from Alabama, Wilbur would feel the fire of that movement and in time join the battle full on.

First, he had to deal with a more pressing personal problem: polio. He'd contracted the plague of the 1950s when he was two years old. By the time he was five, he couldn't walk without the aid of crutches and braces. To get treatment, he had to travel back and forth to the children's hospital in Memphis, a 120-mile round-trip that, since the Coloms didn't have a car, required taking a bus from Ripley to New Albany, then another bus from New Albany to Memphis—all while sitting in the back on segregated buses.

It isn't difficult to understand why Wil Colom, once he recovered from polio (but destined to walk on a left leg that would always be half the size of his right), became a Freedom Rider at the age of thirteen, joining the hundreds of protestors who infiltrated segregated buses and whites-only waiting rooms across the South, demanding integration. Back home in Ripley, he went to jail for swimming in the whites-only swimming pool—three times.

Wilbur's father, Milton, ran a small grocery store in Ripley that he'd opened after years of driving a wholesale food delivery truck. Wilbur began working at the store at age seven and by age nine could run it by himself, including operating the cash register and ordering supplies. That kind of self-reliance extended to his education. His parents had little in the way of formal schooling. Growing up in poverty and the strictures of the Deep South, Milton Colom had just a second-grade education, and Gwendolyn Colom, whom everyone called Gwynn, dropped out in tenth grade when she was pregnant with Wilbur's older brother Rod. But tough circumstances notwithstanding, they were good examples to their children. Milton taught himself to read and write, and Gwynn went back to school to get her high school degree.

The three oldest Colom boys, Rod, Roland, and Wil, attended segregated schools until they were teenagers. In a Mississippi county with a population that was just 17 percent black, that meant the grammar school Wilbur attended as a young boy had hardly any books. He did most of his reading out of church books and other printed material at the Church of Christ, where his father was a deacon.

Wilbur told me that it wasn't until he was thirteen that he read his first "regular" book from cover to cover: *The Last of the Mohicans*, by James Fenimore Cooper.

For all the limitations they had to overcome in the organized school system—and there were many for African American kids growing up in the South in the 1950s and 1960s—Wil and his older brothers persevered. They took charge of their own education: autodidacts of the first order. They largely taught themselves until they graduated from high school. And they didn't stop there. Each went on to college. By the time they were through, Rod Colom had become the first black engineer from Tippah County, Mississippi; Roland Colom had become the county's first black dentist; and Wilbur Colom, after getting his bachelor's degree at Howard University and his law degree from Antioch College School of Law in Washington, D.C., had become Tippah County's first black lawyer.

To honor their father and the strong emphasis he placed on education, the Colom brothers donated funds to establish the Milton Colom Computer Science Room in the library at Jackson State University in

Jackson, Mississippi—quite a tribute to a man whose formal schooling stopped at second grade.

I admire my friend Wilbur's commonsense approach to life. In a lifetime of overcoming barriers that others might have looked at as insurmountable, he's constantly looking forward, refusing to hold grudges. After all he went through in his and America's struggle for true racial equality, I remember him telling me, "I got my civil rights in 1976, then I decided I'd use them to go make some money."

He made good on his pledge. In 1981, barely into his thirties, he became the youngest lawyer in history to argue in front of the U.S. Supreme Court. The case involved a young man who was a nursing student and wanted to take classes at an all-women's college in Mississippi. After the school's single-sex policy was upheld in the lower courts, the case made its way on appeal all the way to the Supreme Court. There, Wilbur stood in front of the highest tribunal in the land and was able to persuade the justices that his client had indeed been discriminated against.

As might be suspected from one who had known discrimination firsthand, Wilbur's legal practice veered toward defending the picked-on and disadvantaged. Shortly after the college case, he defended a thirteen-year-old white boy who had been harassed and abused by a black school teacher, winning a sizeable jury verdict. That was followed by representing a Muslim community that had been denied a permit to build a mosque, resulting in a favorable change in the zoning laws. Many more race- and sex-discrimination cases followed.

Wilbur's brilliant legal career has enabled him to give back in a variety of important ways. The Colom Foundation, the charitable entity he formed with Dorothy, who is a senior chancery court district judge in Columbus, Mississippi, supports any number of worthy causes, including FirstBook, a program Wilbur helped create that has given more than 375,000 to-own books to disadvantaged children throughout the southeastern United States.

I've been fortunate to be able to join Wilbur in a number of projects in Africa, including one called the African Healthy Woman Program that helps provide much-needed mammogram machines and services to growing numbers of African women. It was on the first of our many trips together to Africa that I learned he'd had polio as a youngster—after we'd known each other more than twenty years!

Wil Colom's story speaks volumes about the importance of taking personal responsibility, of not blaming others, of not playing the victim card or blaming the system, of looking for opportunities and not excuses. If you can't walk, do something about it; if you're being discriminated against, do something about it; if you aren't educated, do something about that, too.

The Coloms passed on their love of education to their children.

It was through my friendship with Wilbur that I was introduced to a national civic organization called the 100 Black Men of America. Here is their mission statement: "To educate and empower African-American children and teens."

They look out for kids.

I like the organization's motto: "What they see is what they'll be," meaning that those people whom the youth watch and study—the people they see—will in large measure determine the direction they will choose for their own lives. Role models definitely matter.

Wilbur belongs to the 100 Black Men's chapter in Columbus, Mississippi, and arranged to have me talk about *Autodidactic* to the chapter's youth group called the Protégés. After I gave my presentation, I asked Dennis Erby, the president of the club, if I could join the 100 Black Men.

"Well," he said, skipping right past the whiteness of my skin, "you don't live in Columbus."

"Is that a problem?" I asked. Erby said he wasn't sure, "We'll have to check that out."

He checked it out. There was no restriction to an out-of-stater joining the chapter.

"I guess you're in," said Dennis, making me the first white person in the organization.

(When Dennis Erby was later nominated to be U.S. Marshal for the Northern District of Mississippi, they asked him at his congressional hearing if he belonged to any groups that discriminated racially. He could truthfully answer, "No.")

Thanks to generous support from the Columbus chapter of the 100 Black Men, along with backing from Wilbur Colom, Walter Fleishhacker, and other individuals interested in doing everything possible to support the youth of Mississippi, that initial talk in Columbus in turn led to numerous invitations to speak at schools throughout the state.

16

The Friend

A FEW YEARS INTO my autodidactic phase of life, I sat down at a Starbucks in Palm Desert, California, with Bill Thrasher.

Bill Thrasher, to put it mildly, was a hero of mine. Five years younger than he, I watched from an idol-worshipping vantage point as Thrasher did it all as an athlete. He was All Desert Valley League in football, basketball, and baseball. Everything he did in sports he did well. As the quarterback on the football team, he won the league scoring title his junior year, when the team won nine straight games and went all the way to the California Interscholastic Federation finals in Los Angeles. Everyone in the desert knew who Bill Thrasher was.

The reason we were sitting down at Starbucks was because his fifty-year Indio High School reunion was coming up, and he'd been asked to give a short talk at the event.

Although we had touched base by phone now and then, I had not really kept close track of Bill over the years. He quickly filled me in. After high school, he thought he might play football on the college level, but as great as he was at Indio High, at five foot nine and 160 pounds, he was undersized for the next level. He took up golf, and with his natural athletic ability he became a scratch player and actually made a run at playing professionally, although in the end that didn't turn out either.

Outside of sports, he'd done little with his life. He told me he felt like a failure. He didn't want to talk at the reunion because he didn't think he had anything to say, but felt he had no choice. He was, after all, Bill Thrasher.

The reason he'd come to me was because he wanted help writing his speech. Bill knew that I was a trial lawyer and talked for a living. He knew that if Jimmy knew anything, he knew how to give a talk, and he had heard through the grapevine that I had become a published author. Our relationship, such as it was, had always been a good one. He felt he could ask me this favor without being rejected or embarrassed.

It was as if we were back in high school and he was asking one of the kids who went to class to help him finish his assignment. (The irony wasn't lost on me that if we really were back in high school, I'd be the last person he'd go to for help.)

I looked across the table at a man I'd held on a pedestal for half a century. Could this be happening? When I lent a sympathetic ear, he proceeded to bare his soul to me about his regrets. He confided that he wished he would have applied himself in school and gotten a decent education. He'd gone through his life never confident in conversations. He wasn't a good reader and as a result didn't feel as if he knew much of anything.

He talked about high school and the cakewalk it had been for him because he was good looking and a top athlete. He remembered how he got a C in chemistry because the chemistry teacher lived next door to the football coach and Bill needed the passing grade to be eligible for the team.

"When I came home from school I'd throw the books on the couch and the next morning I'd take them back to school," he confessed. "I don't think they ever got opened."

He had a girlfriend—the best-looking girl in the school, naturally—who was a straight-A student and could have helped him a lot, but he wasn't interested.

He mused on the irony that as quarterback, he memorized the playbook word for word. He knew it backward and forward. "If a lineman ever forgot his assignment, I could tell him what it was on the spot," he told me. "I knew all the blocking assignments, everything everyone was supposed to do. I just took it upon myself; I wanted to know every play. If anyone was confused, I wanted to be able to help them. But I couldn't crack a book of geometry. I didn't think it was important. Everything was ball. It was all I thought about, all I lived for."

He credited a strict father with teaching him the key lessons in life—honesty, hard work, and dependability. He'd spent his life doing manual labor and working as a golf instructor. In his late sixties, he was teaching golf, running the cart barn, and caddying for high-end players at an upscale resort in Dana Point, California. A good, steady job, but he felt inferior because of his lack of an education. If the conversation wasn't about sports, he felt completely inadequate.

I told him, of course I'd help him with his talk, although my conjecture was that it wouldn't matter what he said because the only reason people go to reunions is to see you as you were, not as you are.

Before he left, I reached into my briefcase and handed him a copy of *Autodidactic*.

"I want you to read this," I told him.

"Why?" he asked.

"Just read it and then let's talk," I said. "You asked me for a favor, now I'm asking you for one. It's not very long. Please read it."

Bill Thrasher wasn't in the habit of reading books. But he read that one. We met the next day at the same Starbucks.

He said, "Jimmy, your book was written for me.

"What you wrote hit me like a sledgehammer. I need a vocabulary, I need to understand words, I need to learn. I never have. All these years I've felt inadequate. I never dreamed there was a way out of my ignorance."

I couldn't quite believe what I was hearing. My childhood hero was reciting to me precisely the thesis statement from my book. He wanted to take responsibility for his own education. Now. Before it was too late.

For a variety of reasons, Bill had always thought learning and literacy were out of his reach. He was convinced he wasn't bright enough. He was a dummy. A dumb jock. That assessment had been drummed into him at some point—much as it had to me early on—and it stayed with him all his life.

Now, he was being told it wasn't up to anybody else. It was up to him.

He asked me what books he could start reading that would lay a good foundation. I reached in my pocket and pulled out a Barnes & Noble gift card and gave it to him. I then opened my little book and showed him my list of books I recommended. He made a goal to read them all. Fiction. Nonfiction. History. Sociology. Politics. Philosophy.

We began to talk on a regular basis. It was as if Bill had opened the door to a room in his own home he never knew existed. That he could expand his vocabulary and his mind with facts and information was to him almost not to be believed. That he could write his thoughts down was unbelievable.

He confessed he had hardly written anything in his life. He recalled a painful memory from high school when his beautiful girlfriend went away one summer. Every day she wrote Bill a letter, and he never wrote her back. Not because he was an unfeeling louse, but because he felt there was no way he could respond in kind. He could never match the words she was putting down on paper.

"I didn't know how to write, I couldn't create a conversation on a piece of paper," he said. "I could write I love you and that was it. So that's all I'd do."

That high school girlfriend went on to Stanford and married the star quarterback, while Bill dropped out of college when football didn't work out. Learning was for others.

But not anymore. Now, learning was for Bill Thrasher. He turned off his TV. No more all-day football weekends.

As his vocabulary increased, so did his thirst for information. He wanted to know about history, about what makes things tick, about the lives of great people. "We have giant people we look up to, who went through life just like us, and we can learn from them and take advantage of all they went through by reading about them," he exclaimed.

Bill's older brother, fifteen years his senior, had studied hard in high school, went on to college, and enjoyed a career as a psychology professor. That brother had tried to steer Bill toward language and books when he was young but to no avail. The result was a distant relationship throughout their lives because they had little common ground.

After becoming an autodidact, Bill reached out to his brother, who was now retired, and in their leisure they began having long conversations about all sorts of subjects, cementing a bond that might have been formed years before.

"We have become closer because he's a reader and I'm a reader," Bill told me. "We can talk about things we couldn't talk about before. The nice thing about it is now I can sit down and be in his world."

Bill Thrasher is a tough guy, an athlete, a man's man. He doesn't cry easily. But tears come to his eyes when he talks about the change in his life brought about by literacy and learning. He reads more books now in a month than he read in his first sixty years of life. And enjoys it immensely. "I go all around the world now, never leaving my apartment, and see things," he said. "It's fascinating."

His gratitude to me has been effusive. No one in my life has thanked me more often and sincerely than Bill Thrasher. All because I handed him a copy of my book.

"Why didn't I have this book in high school!?" he whispered to me the last time we talked. "I'm the guy this book was written for!"

17

Mentors

BEFORE I FINISHED WRITING this book, I asked a number of trusted friends to read the manuscript. Several of them made the suggestion that I ought to add at least one chapter, if not several chapters, setting forth what advice I would give to educators, parents, politicians, and other opinion makers on what to do to improve education in general and literacy in particular. If I were to do that, now would be the appropriate time.

I decided not to.

Although I have been traveling around the country and the world to speak about education and literacy for the past ten years, and I've written two other books on the topic, I still do not feel that I'm qualified to give advice to professionals on how to do their jobs. I've had personal experiences that I'm happy to share, but to do justice to the topic of giving advice would require a lot more study and research by me. In other words, it's beyond my pay grade. I have my observations from my travels, but to sit down and tell the professionals what to do isn't what I'm trying to accomplish with this book. What I am trying to do is share experiences that have been plentiful and rich, hopefully to inspire educators, but not tell them didactically what to do. That's already been tried by those who wrote No Child Left Behind, Race to the Top, Common Core, ad nauseum.

What I am an expert on, and something I would really like to share before I close this book, is the incredible impact mentors have had on me and my education. In this chapter, I will introduce you to several of the mentors I've had in my life. Each is unique in his or her own right, but there is a common thread in the tapestry of their life experiences: each one is an autodidact, a lifetime learner, and remarkably predisposed to share with others what they learned in their lifetimes both professionally and personally.

Having a mentor is an experience to be cherished—exceeded only, perhaps, by being a mentor yourself and in some small way passing on the great gift I have been given. Nothing thrills me more than the opportunity to sit down one-on-one with an eager student who wants to pick my brain and learn from my successes and, yes, my many failures. There's an old Indian saying that you've not really learned anything unless you've shared it. I was very moved when watching the service for former president George H. W. Bush and hearing his philosophy that no life is worth living unless you have been involved in the service of others. That, too, is a common thread that runs through the people I am proud to introduce you to.

Richard P. Parkinson, MD

When I was a boy, my physician father used to get in his car on weekends and drive two hours to the medical center at UCLA so that he could scrub up and watch a surgeon named Franklin Ashley close up wounds.

In the world of plastic surgery, Dr. Ashley was a legend, renowned for not only saving the careers of Hollywood movie stars with his careful incisions that left no visible marks and scars, but also for reconstructing the faces and bodies of Vietnamese and African children maimed by poverty and war. He was the best of the best. And my father, Richard P. Parkinson, MD, wanted to learn from him.

For years, Dad made that weekend trek from Indio to Los Angeles so that he could stand next to Dr. Ashley and study how to close wounds. He became so good at it that word spread throughout the desert communities where we lived: if you get any kind of cut, you want to have Dr. Parkinson sew you up because he won't leave a scar. Hearing that talk brought me immense pride.

It also provided me with my first glimpse into the importance of mentors.

The dictionary defines mentor, when used as a noun, as "an experienced and trusted adviser." Used as a verb, it means "to advise and train."

Mentors set the course and show the way. Most importantly, they focus with laser intensity on you as an individual. Their value and impact cannot be overstated.

When talking to high school students about the importance of taking responsibility for their own education, I stress that one of the best ways to do that is by reaching out to mentors who know things that they don't.

Until you admit what you don't know, you'll never learn what you need to know.

This requires a good dose of humility, by the way. I learned that from my first mentor, Susan Greene.

Sue Greene

I met Sue during my first year of college. She and her twin sister, Randi, lived in a nearby dorm. I had two weekly essays I had to do for my English class, and due to the fact that my keyboarding skills were practically nonexistent and that she was off-the-charts cute, I asked Sue if she'd type them for me. To my surprise, she took pity on me and agreed—only to hand the papers back to me the next day.

"I can't type these," she said.

"Why not?" I asked.

"Because they make no sense, they're not properly written, there's no punctuation."

Fortunately, after a good bit of begging, she agreed to sit down with me and show me how to put a period at the end of a sentence, how to turn sentences into paragraphs, and how to turn paragraphs into a coherent message. She taught me the basics of good writing. With time, I was producing good enough papers that she condescended to type them for me.

It was the beginning of a beautiful relationship. Three years later, the smartest, prettiest, kindest woman I've ever seen became my wife. She's the best thing that ever happened to me and continues to teach me something I don't know every single day. As great as her lessons were about writing, her lessons about how to care for and treat people are that much greater.

During my formative years, I was blessed with a succession of wonderful mentors; people who gave me instruction and directed me to paths I didn't even know existed.

My career as a lawyer might never have gotten off the ground if not for a law professor who went beyond for me, igniting an aptitude and appreciation for the law I didn't know I possessed.

Monroe McKay

Monroe McKay was hardly the typical law professor. A cowboy who grew up in rural northern Utah, he was more John Wayne than Socrates. For some reason he took a liking to me when I was in my third and final year at the BYU law school and hired me as his research assistant for a class he taught on administrative law. My assignment was to research cases that were in the curriculum and brief him on them before he taught the class.

For these briefings, we developed a routine of walking across the street from the law school to the BYU student center, where we would find a table and have a donut and soft drink while we discussed the cases.

These informal, unconventional sessions (it wasn't exactly routine for law professors to take donut breaks with their students) opened new horizons for me. Monroe had a brilliant mind. He got his law degree at the University of Chicago before practicing law in Phoenix, Arizona, where among other things he was second chair on the case that resulted in the Miranda Law, mandating that police officers need to read people their rights when arresting them.

But for all his intellect, he had a way of talking about the law that made it not just understandable but fascinating. He indulged my every question and fed my curiosity. He was conversant about all aspects of the law and generous with his time.

A light went on for me. A fog lifted. I'd been in law school for three years, and for the first time I started to make some sense of what we were studying. Up to my donut breaks with Professor McKay, I'd sit in class after class taught in the adversarial Socratic Method, where the professor plays the role of a boot-camp drill sergeant, answering questions with more questions, and the students pray they don't rile him (or her) any more than they already have. There are no frequent tests in this system and virtually no feedback. It's essentially learning through intimidation and fear. I did not thrive in these sparring sessions.

Monroe changed all that. He brought the subject matter to life. Sitting there one-on-one with him I realized I wasn't a law student with no skills who couldn't learn. It wasn't that I didn't have the intellectual tools to handle the material; it was that I'd never had it properly presented and explained so I could get my mind around it. From Professor McKay I learned how to learn the law.

I didn't attend a single session of the administrative law class that semester. Attendance wasn't mandatory, and I already knew the material backward and forward. When I took the final exam I not only got the highest score in the class, it turned out it was the highest score ever given in the law school's history.

Since in three years of law school I'd never scored nearly so high on a final, the administration suspected foul play, causing something of a ruckus. They held up my grades while they conducted an investigation to see if—or how—I'd cheated. In the end, after talking to the professor and to me, they came to the correct conclusion that I really did know the subject matter inside and out.

A few months later, after I graduated, I took the California bar exam, a notoriously difficult test with a pass rate of less than 50 percent. But I'd been taught at the feet of a master, and I aced it. All those times in the student center talking with Professor McKay really paid off. From those sessions, I learned and mastered everything there was to learn and master about administrative law, and it showed when I took the test. In studying for the bar, I took the same approach. I knew it wasn't okay to know 50 percent of the material, or 75 percent; I needed to know 100 percent. That was the way I prepared, and it paid off handsomely.

My only regret is that I didn't run into Monroe McKay earlier in law school. He brought the law to life and made learning its many nuances a pleasurable pursuit rather than an intimidating experience.

Monroe McKay stayed just one more year on the faculty at BYU, until President Jimmy Carter appointed him to the federal bench. He was assigned to sit on the U.S. Court of Appeals for the Tenth District with headquarters in Denver, Colorado, a position he's now held for more than forty years.

The bond we formed in one year of law school together never wavered. After he became a federal judge, we continued to talk regularly on the phone and took trips together to Africa and Argentina. I have fond memories of sitting at a corner café in Buenos Aires and spending hours talking about constitutional law—Monroe still teaching and I still learning. The interest that good man took in my development as a lawyer and as a human being is one of the great blessings of my life.

Tom Anderson

I had another great mentor at my first law office. Tom Anderson was an outstanding attorney and a man of high principle, with an extraordinary ability to relate to all people, including those on the opposite side of the case. I've never known a more ethical man. He treated everyone fairly and with respect. Most of all, me. During lunchtime, when we'd break for a sandwich, he'd take the time to talk to me about the best way to try cases, and how to talk to juries. When he'd try cases, he would take me along to observe, and afterward he would explain his strategy and tactics. He trained me like that for a full year, until one day he handed me a case of my own and uttered seven of the most meaningful words anyone has ever said to me: "I trust you to try this case."

It's incalculable how valuable that was in shaping my self-confidence and launching my future.

Rod Baseshore

Sometimes a mentor will appear when you least expect it. That's what happened with me when my second law partner suggested we run an ad on Spanish television to solicit clients, and since I was fluent in Spanish, I should do the ad.

I agreed that it was a good idea, but I didn't feel comfortable filming a TV commercial without some training. When my daughter Krista was in high school, she had a legendary drama teacher named Rod Baseshore. I made a donation to the Circle Theater Mr. Baseshore ran at Indio High, and then I reached out to him and asked if he'd be willing to do me a favor and help me get ready for my television spot.

He couldn't have been more gracious. He invited me out to his ranch on a Monday night. I expected a short session, and that would be the end of it. Turned out I went almost every Monday night for the next five years. We became great friends as he taught me everything you could learn about speech, about debate, about drama, about reading your audience.

I'll never forget the first thing he said to me. "We need to start by telling each other the truth," he said. "Do you want me to tell you how you come across to people the first time they meet you?"

"Sure," I answered, not at all sure I wanted to know the answer.

"You come across like an a—hole."

Well, now he had my attention ...

"I'm not saying you are an a—hole," he continued. "But that's how you come across. That's how you came across when I first met you. Two minutes into talking to you I found that you're kind, considerate, and so forth, but that wasn't my first impression."

He explained why. "You're six foot three and 250 pounds, and when you meet people you immediately straighten up and look down on them. That makes people very uncomfortable. Are you aware of that?"

I absolutely was not.

He said I should start paying attention; take my cue from others, put myself in their shoes, understand what they might be thinking.

He taught me the importance of making people comfortable. When you're in front of an audience, he advised, you should pause for a moment before you begin speaking—give the audience an opportunity to settle into their seats. And always take note of where people are sitting so you can determine whether you need to raise or lower your voice so they can best hear you.

We read the scene from the play *Inherit the Wind* that replicates the courtroom debate between William Jennings Bryan and Clarence Darrow in the famous Scopes Monkey Trial. He showed me ten different ways to act the same scene. I had no idea how many ways you could say the lines and how differently they could sound with a change in emphasis and inflection.

The first time I had a trial after we started working together, I came to Rod with my closing argument. After I read it, I asked him what he thought. He answered by asking his wife, Judy, to come into the room. "Put your papers away," he said, "and just tell Judy what your case is about."

I did as he asked, and when I was finished, he said, "Don't give the closing argument you read to me. Talk to the jury like you just talked to Judy."

Sure enough, I did it that way at the trial, and the jury came back and gave me what I asked for.

That only happens in movies when Paul Newman is the lawyer.

Rod Baseshore opened to me the power of just being me. I learned so much from him it was unbelievable. More than once, I tried to pay him. He always refused my money. He said, "I'm a teacher; teaching's what I do. The fact you want to learn is the price of admission." I probably owe more to Rod in terms of my public persona than anybody on the planet.

Grant Fitts

Of all the mentors who shaped and molded me as a young lawyer, none was any more generous or unexpected than Grant Fitts.

By the time I made his acquaintance, Grant Fitts was a success many times over. He'd started out dirt poor in the little town of Shady Grove, Alabama, and became one of the most powerful businessmen in America, the founder and guiding partner/CEO of Gulf United, a company head-quartered in Dallas that was traded on the New York Stock Exchange and included television stations, airlines, insurance companies, and a number of other businesses in its portfolio.

Prior to that, he had practiced law in Birmingham, Alabama. He graduated top of his class at Harvard Law School and spent more than a decade in private legal practice, honing the skills of negotiation and preparation that would serve him so well in business.

My father and Grant were friends, so when I was considering a career change as a young lawyer my dad arranged for me to meet with Grant and get his advice. I honestly can't remember much of what he had to say about my changing law firms. What I do remember is what he taught me about focus and preparation.

Grant was a unique individual, an absolute loner. He lived in a 20,000-square-foot house by himself with four full-time servants on three acres. From time to time he would call me and invite me to fly to Dallas and play a few rounds of golf with him and visit. He would send his chauffeur to the airport, and we'd play golf. Then at night after dinner, we'd talk in his study for hours at a time. He would discuss his cases as a lawyer, the strategy he used, the outcomes, what the other side argued, and I would sit there mesmerized by these stories.

One night he asked me how I structured my closing argument.

I stammered for an answer, but when it was clear I really didn't have one, he pointed to a shelf in his library and said, "Hand me that book."

It was a copy of *Famous American Jury Speeches* collected and edited by Frederick C. Hicks and published in 1925. It was worn and obviously well used, with scotch tape holding the spine in place.

Grant opened to a chapter about Clarence Darrow's famous closing argument in the Leopold murder case.

"Read it," he said. "And we'll talk in the morning."

It took me until past midnight to read it all. Clarence Darrow talked to the jury for twelve hours straight, pleading for the lives of his young clients, Nathan Leopold and Richard Loeb, both teenagers, who had taken the life of a fourteen-year-old boy in a case that riveted the nation back in 1924. In print form, the closing argument took ninety-eight pages.

In the book's margins, Grant had handwritten numerous notes, which I paid close attention to because I knew I'd be grilled about them at breakfast.

The next morning as we talked, I had the book in front of me and Grant didn't. And yet he discussed the case in amazing detail, often quoting what he had written in those margin notes word for word. More amazing was the fact he'd made those notes when he studied the case in law school almost fifty years before. He hadn't pulled that book off the shelf in decades!

The next night Grant had me read the prosecution's closing argument, delivered by Robert Crowe. "It's even better," he said.

The next morning we spent four hours talking about that, his memory equally sharp.

When I complimented him on his incredible recall, he insisted his memory wasn't any better or worse than anyone else's. The reason he could recall things so well, he insisted, was because of how much attention he'd paid in the first place.

What you focus on—really focus on—you won't soon forget.

When you read something, don't move on until you understand the subject matter. Read it again, and again, and again. Don't do it halfway. Stay with it until you've figured it out. Focus. Focus. Focus. That's what Grant Fitts taught me. A light went on in my head. After what he taught me, I never wanted to leave a discussion until I understood completely what was being said.

He told me that before he tried a case or went into a business meeting, he would take out a piece of paper and write out exactly what he was going to say. He would imagine conversations and questions and scenarios that might or might not come up. He was ready for anything. And when you're prepared for anything, your chances of success rise exponentially.

My favorite example of Grant Fitts–style preparation is when he decided he was going to take up golf, recognizing how useful playing the game can be for business relationships. He was a full-grown adult at this point and knew nothing about the sport; he hadn't swung a club in his life. To learn, he acquired a number of teaching books, read them all from cover to cover, and practiced his swing for hours in front of a full-length mirror in total privacy at home. Then, the first time he played on an actual golf course, he broke one hundred for eighteen holes, a remarkable accomplishment for a first-time player. He went on to develop a first-rate game and for twenty years became a regular playing companion of golfing legend Ben Hogan.

In my development as a lawyer, I added what Grant Fitts taught me about preparation to what Rod Baseshore taught me about presentation, anchored by the foundation laid by Monroe McKay and Tom Anderson. It didn't guarantee I would win every case, but walking into the courtroom standing on my mentors' shoulders always made me think I would.

18

Rewards from the Road

IN NEARLY TEN YEARS of traveling around the country and other parts of the world to spread my message of self-education and literacy, I've stood on many stages and gazed out at thousands and thousands of students.

But it's not the crowds that stay with me and keep me coming back; it's the individual.

I wasn't prepared for my reaction. I suppose if I'm honest about my ego, which some have suggested is quite sizeable, my expectation was for more of a rock-star–like reception; in the beginning I envisioned that the sound of my voice and the power of my words would inspire the masses to rise up and read!

That, of course, hasn't happened. More than a one-hour talk is required to ignite a full-blown revolution.

What has happened is an unexpected opportunity for me to see each student as a separate entity, each one a fully functioning human being in his or her own right, quite apart from the throng.

It begins when I stand at the entrance to the auditorium where I'm scheduled to speak. I arrive at the school in plenty of time before any of the kids show up. (Want to see real enthusiasm? That comes before the speech ever happens. You should see how excited the kids are to get out of class for an assembly.) Stationed at the door of the auditorium, I shake the hand of every kid coming in. Some of them shy away, but I insist on making contact with each individual. I want them to understand that this is personal, that everyone matters.

This has led to a number of extraordinary encounters with students after the assembly is over. Encounters that have touched my heart as I've gained an appreciation for the real fears and difficulties students often confront as they're pursuing their education.

I'd finished my talk at Cedar City High School in Cedar City, Utah, when a student wearing basketball shorts and a t-shirt—an unusual outfit considering it was the middle of winter and the temperature outside was below freezing—approached me.

More unusual yet was the question he asked me: "Were you lying?"

I wasn't sure I'd heard that right. "What did you say?" I asked.

"I want to know if you were lying when you said everybody can make it."

"I absolutely meant it," I assured him, and then encouraged him to explain why he thought I wasn't telling the truth.

He told me his story: he'd been sent to live in foster care with a Cedar City family after he and his siblings had been taken from the single mother who was paying far more attention to her drug habit than she was to her children. The family had lived fifty miles away in St. George, Utah, where the climate is much warmer, which explained his wardrobe. All he owned in the way of pants were the basketball shorts, which hung mid-calf, and his only shirts were short-sleeved t-shirts.

I looked at him in amazement. It was so easy to judge this book by its cover, thinking here was just another rebellious nonconformist teenager, when the reality was far different. He didn't have anything else to wear.

"What chance do I have?" he wanted to know. What hope was there for someone already so abused?

It broke my heart. After we talked, I talked to his teacher, Mrs. Esplin. "Please make sure this kid gets a dictionary," I said as I pulled out twenty dollars. Then I pulled out some more money and added, "And some winter clothes."

At the end of the semester, I got a call from Mrs. Esplin. That boy, she told me, had gone from a D-minus to a B-plus.

Stories like that will keep me going until I drop.

I've found it amazing in my travels how much a kind word or just a touch can matter. I was at Rancho Mirage High School in California on the outskirts of Palm Springs, when a young girl came up to me after my talk. I'd spoken to fourteen hundred kids over a two-day span. Even though I shook hands with all of them, by the end of that much talking they were a blur.

I was exhausted, catching my breath, when a Hispanic girl shyly approached me. We walked away a few feet for some privacy, and she proceeded to tell me her life was falling apart, her parents had just ordered her out of the house. Forget literacy and reading—she didn't know where she was going to live.

Out of the corner of my eye, I saw an African American girl heading toward us. She'd noticed what was happening. She introduced herself, told us her own sad story—pregnant at fourteen, miscarried the baby, got off drugs, and now she was back in school, determined to see it through and graduate. She sensed the girl I was talking to needed to hear that.

"Let me give you a hug," she said, and took that young Hispanic girl in her arms and embraced her.

The English teacher came over. Her jaw dropped at what she was seeing. Kids still care.

At that same school, I had lunch with the drama teacher, Kelly Newhouse, and her husband, Ron. As we ate, I noticed kids going back and forth to the refrigerator in an adjoining room. I asked what was going on. Kelly told me they kept the fridge stocked with mac and cheese so the kids who might not have brought any food to school would know they wouldn't have to go hungry.

"Who pays for that?" I asked.

"My husband and I."

Now my jaw dropped.

Experiences like that have caused me to recognize that I'm not always, or even very often, talking to kids headed to Harvard. My assemblies aren't packed with fifteen hundred Jimmy Parkinsons just waiting to be inspired. Many of them are facing hard issues. They're just trying to make it. I'm not so delusional that I think my talk is going to turn the light on for the next Nelson Mandela. I just want to be one of many who touch the life of somebody for good, and maybe the synergistic help of all of us will make a difference.

More often than not, I am the recipient of compassion and caring. I'll not soon forget my visit to a Locke High School in Watts, smack in the heart of south-central Los Angeles—a place that has never been mistaken for Beverly Hills.

My daughter Krista was friends with the principal, Peggy Guiterrez, and set up the appearance. Going in, I thought I'd be speaking to an audience of 100 percent African Americans. But I was surprised to find that half of the students were Hispanic, most of them coming from Central

America, not Mexico. Principal Guiterrez thanked me for coming and then warned me that only half of my audience would understand what I was saying. I said, "Nonsense, bring them in," and after everyone was seated I spoke to them in Spanish for an hour.

After the assembly, I asked for questions. A girl in the back raised her hand and said she had a comment rather than a question. I braced for what she might say, and then she surprised me by saying this: "Nobody comes here and gives us anything. But you did. You came and gave us this program and now you're giving us a copy of your book. Somebody needs to give you a thank you and a hug, and that somebody ought to be me."

I said, "Go for it," so she marched onto the stage and gave me a hug and sat down. It remains one of the most touching things I've had happen to me.

At many of the schools I visit, I sponsor an essay contest. I give a cash award for the top essays, one hundred dollars for first place, seventy-five for second, and fifty for third. Enough to get their attention. Usually, the students receive a copy of my book at the assembly. After they read the book, they write their essays, and their teachers pick the winners, and I send the checks.

My hope, of course, is that this will motivate the students into taking responsibility for their own education.

During one of my trips to Mississippi, I stopped by to talk with Jermaine Taylor, the principal of West Point High School. I'd given my assembly there previously, and we had become good friends. West Point is 98 percent African American—in sharp contrast to fifty years ago when it was almost all white. The school is an example of the unfortunate self-segregation going on throughout much of the Deep South.

Mr. Taylor can point to a photograph hanging in the main hall that helps tell the story. In 1971, the photo of the graduating seniors shows an almost all white student body. In 1972, the year West Point High got serious about obeying the federal government mandate to integrate, more than 50 percent of the students are black—including Jermaine Taylor's mother. In every photograph since 1972, the percentage of black students has increased. Today, most white kids who live in the West Point High School boundaries are attending private schools instead.

What this says about humankind's ability to move on and learn from the past is a matter for social scientists, not an accidental academic. But the reality is that the West Point High demographics in the twenty-first century show a high percentage of predominantly African American students living in pretty tough circumstances, most of them below the poverty line.

During my visit, Mr. Taylor asked a student to escort me to another part of the school. As we were walking through the halls, the black student looked at me and said, "You don't remember me, do you?"

I searched my memory. There was something familiar about her.

"Tell me who you are?" I asked.

"I was the winner of your essay contest last time you were here," she said.

Then it came back to me. I remembered her essay and how well written it was. I congratulated her again and asked her how her life was going.

It would have been impossible for me to be prepared for what she told me.

Over the past year, she said, her mother, suffering from some sort of breakdown, burned down their house and killed her grandfather who was inside.

Just another day in the life of a kid trying to graduate from high school.

But she was soldiering on, she assured me. That essay contest, she said, had inspired her to buckle down more than ever in school, even despite the tragedy that was her family life. She had won a scholarship to Alcorn State and was planning to enroll there as a freshman as soon as she graduated. Thank goodness, young people are resilient.

The thirst to learn is universal. It knows no borders, it embraces every culture, every social strata. Rich and poor, black and white, old and young. On one of my international speaking trips, I was invited to talk to an entrepreneurial class taught by a friend, Clark Arrington, at the Julius Nyerera University in Dar es Salaam, Tanzania.

After I spoke to these budding businessmen about being autodidacts, I asked, as I often do, if anyone had a question.

Every hand in the room went up. I'd never seen that before. Three hundred hands at once!

On that same African trip, I talked to a group of doctors in The Gambia, one of Africa's poorest countries. I was part of a group looking at helping implement a breast-cancer-detection system in the country. I was asked to address about fifty doctors, about forty of whom came from Cuba.

Describing the reception I got from the Cuban audience as frosty would not be doing it justice. There just wasn't a whole lot of enthusiasm for an American—from a capitalist country, an enemy—standing in front of them about to dispense wisdom.

I looked at a woman doctor in the front row and asked her, in English, if she spoke Spanish. "Of course I do, I'm Cuban," she said.

"Would you prefer I talked in Spanish?" I asked.

She said yes and offered to help me. But I didn't need help. I'd learned Spanish in Argentina as a young man and had done my best to keep up with it ever since. For the next forty-five minutes, I spoke to the group in Spanish. The change in the reception was night to day. Suddenly, I felt completely welcomed. Afterward, the Cuban doctors surrounded me and we talked for over an hour.

What was the difference? All I can ascribe it to was my speaking their language. They knew I cared enough to speak to them the way they speak, and not just with words but in referencing their poets, their literature, and their culture.

I think about that experience wherever I go—the importance of speaking to others in a way that says you care who they are, you appreciate their struggle, their culture, their triumphs, and what they're going through.

Over and over in my travels, I've seen that showing respect is the best way to motivate and inspire others. I believe that is the key to education. It starts with someone who cares. The people who have taught me that valuable lesson teach it through their actions, not their words.

People like the Reverend Jody Hill.

Jody is pastor of Ripley Presbyterian Church in Ripley, Mississippi, and an administrator at Blue Mountain College, a small regional school located in Blue Mountain, Mississippi.

Reverend Hill and I became acquainted when I was scheduling schools to speak to in northern Mississippi. Jody was an easy convert to my cause. As soon as he learned that my objective was to improve literacy, he jumped on board with both feet, facilitating my visits to Ripley High School and Falkner High School.

At each school, he stood up first and got the crowd excited. I've yet to see anyone with more enthusiasm who could relate better with young people. By the time he was finished introducing me, even I thought I was a big deal. I marveled at this man's passion and charisma. I learned he'd graduated from the University of Mississippi and then worked in his family's business before answering a call to study for the ministry. As a football player at Ole Miss he was teammates with Chucky Mullins, who was paralyzed in a game and handled his adversity so heroically that it inspired all who knew him. Jody wrote a bestselling book, *38: The Chucky Mullins Effect*, about finding triumph in tragedy.

He told me he felt it was his calling to do all he could to help lift kids out of tough circumstances and put them on the right path. He teaches young people to have good Christian standards and values, and rare is the day that passes when he doesn't emphasize that the best way to find success is through education.

So I'm not alone. My voice is one in a large national chorus of like-minded crusaders who see literacy and learning as the key to happy, satisfied people and a cohesive, progressive society.

My hope—my goal, my quest, my passion—is to further that cause the best way I know how. For me, that means focusing on one message—to encourage all within the sound of my voice to assume responsibility for their own education. No matter where you are, no matter what your circumstances, it will pay untold dividends.

19

The Future

AS I TRAVEL TO schools throughout the country and gaze out at audiences full of youthful faces, I find myself looking for the Bill Thrashers. Where is he? Or her? How can I reach them? How can I ignite a love for learning and literature RIGHT NOW that will pay dividends for a lifetime?

The more I immerse myself in this cause, the more I realize I'm far from alone. Many, many others are bound by the same desire. They give so much. Bill and Melinda Gates have donated $3.4 billion to education efforts, including a sizeable amount to see if smaller schools are the answer (to mixed results). Former New York City mayor Michael Bloomberg pledged $375 million to help students from lower-income backgrounds get into college. (Mr. Bloomberg is a major sponsor of charter schools in New York City; they are proving to be very successful.) Facebook founder Mark Zuckerberg and his wife, Priscilla Chan, gave $20 million to an early-childhood literacy program. Country singer Dolly Parton has distributed more than one hundred million books to young readers since implementing her Imagination Library program in 1995 as a tribute to her father who never learned to read and write. Every child enrolled in the program receives a book a month until they enter kindergarten. In 2018, Imagination Library was distributing one million books a month. The spirit of Andrew Carnegie lives on!

The list goes on and on. Celebrities the likes of Will Smith, Andre Agassi, and Magic Johnson have built schools for at-risk youth. In the summer of 2018, basketball star LeBron James opened his I Promise school in his hometown of Akron, Ohio. The inaugural class was composed of 240 third- and fourth-graders identified as below grade level in reading proficiency. With time, the public school will expand to grades K–8, focusing entirely on at-risk youth. Beyond providing state-of-the-art facilities, the school offers what are called wraparound services for struggling families, things like a food pantry, job and family services, help with housing, even a seven-week summer camp so kids will avoid the summer slide and won't get into trouble when school is out.

As with so many others who choose to champion education causes, the impetus for LeBron James to build and fund the school can be traced directly back to the limitations he faced as a child. Growing up in poverty, raised by a single mother, he could easily have become a casualty of the system, just another dropout. In fourth grade, long before he would become a household name, he missed eighty-three days of school because his mother didn't have a car and they lived too far to walk (it's why every kid at his school gets a bicycle). He barely squeaked by until basketball saved him in high school. When he became prosperous, he vowed to help as many kids as he could avoid the kind of tough circumstances that get in the way of a quality education. "Everything they're going through, I know," he said in a tweet when the I Promise school opened. "I know these kids basically more than they know themselves."

As an added incentive for the I Promise students, James has guaranteed that everyone who graduates from the program will have their tuition paid at the University of Akron.

Particularly eye-opening—and encouraging—to me was the resolution passed in 2018 by the NAACP that said the venerable civil rights organization, in a reversal of its previous stands, would look at charter schools as something that might help improve educational parity for the nation's children of color. Further, the NAACP announced it would partner with The Church of Jesus Christ of Latter-day Saints—the church I affiliate with—in education reform. That willingness to look at the situation through new eyes is a healthy sign. If the NAACP can say to teachers' unions, "Why don't we give charter schools a chance?"—if it can say, "We'll work with the LDS Church"—then that's like sunshine after a heavy rainstorm.

My hope is that others will take the cue from the NAACP and consider new ways to problem solve. Cooperation is absolutely vital to reform. Taking sides and staking out turf has no place when a young person's schooling hangs in the balance. That reminds me of Albert Shanker, who was president of the American Federation of Teachers from 1974 through 1997. During a difficult contract negotiation that threatened a teacher walkout, Shanker was asked why he wasn't considering the needs of the students. He replied, "When school children start paying union dues, that is when I'll start representing the interests of school children."

It's time for the rhetoric to morph from identifying our differences to an understanding that we're all in it together.

My many travels through America's schools have allowed me to arrive at a couple of conclusions:

Number One: the American educational system works. Not as well as we'd like it to, but it's not as bad as our critics think it is. There is so much that is good and effective about the way our children learn. The question isn't, "How do we fix it?" The question is, "How do we make it better?"

Number Two: the great thinkers, planners, and philanthropists, people like Mike Benson, Greg Hughes, Dusty Heuston, Richard Pimentel, Doug Cervi, Michael Bloomberg, Bill Gates, and so many others I have already mentioned, are all working hard to come up with solutions. They are out there, constantly tinkering, innovating, improving, and there are legions of them. For every principal like Pimentel I can tell you about a Monica Rodriguez, who works day and night at Indio High School to give kids great educational opportunities, or a Jermaine Taylor at West Point High School, whose concern for his largely disadvantaged student body is almost palpable. For every teacher like Cervi I can give you Dana Esplin from Cedar City, Utah, who after she raised her family decided to become a teacher because she loves English, and she loves kids.

The list of these great, caring educators goes on and on and on. There's Ely Juaregui at Desert Hot Springs High School in the Palm Springs area of California. During the Christmas holidays one year I was sitting in my condo in Utah when the phone rang. Ely Juaregui introduced himself and said he wanted to talk to me about my program. He'd seen a copy of my book *Autodidactic* on the shelf of an English teacher friend of his who taught at another high school. He pulled it down and read it and thought, *This is exactly what my students need to hear.*

It turned out Mr. Juaregui was part of a program called AVID, an acronym that stands for Advancement Via Individual Determination. AVID's stated mission is "To close the achievement gap by preparing students for college readiness and success in the global society." AVID was founded in California in 1980 by Mary Catherine Swanson, a high school English teacher. In the years since it has expanded to include chapters in forty-seven states. Students who enroll in AVID start their freshman year together and stay as a group all the way through graduation, under the mentorship of one teacher who oversees the group. The emphasis is on the individual and the effort made by that individual. Autodidactism, in other words.

Mr. Juaregui asked if I could come and talk to his students. We quickly arranged a date. I thought it was telling that when I told Ely about the essay contest I like to sponsor, offering cash prizes to the top three essays, he got back to me and said his students wanted to write the essays, but wondered if instead of a competition, could I donate the prize money to fund a field trip for the entire class to visit a university and see what college life was all about. I agreed, and later that year the AVID students at Desert Hot Springs rode a chartered bus to Los Angeles, where they spent the day at UCLA.

As I got to know Ely Juaregui, I understood where his drive to encourage kids, especially those coming from poorer circumstances, came from. His father was a waiter who emigrated from Mexico; his mother picked carrots in the fields in the Coachella Valley. He knew the only way he'd get an education was to join the army and let the GI Bill take care of it. Shortly after he joined, the army sent him to Iraq. He happened to be assigned to the unit that shot down the first missile launched by Saddam Hussein when U.S. troops invaded Iraq in 2003. Upon his return, true to his plan, Ely got his bachelor's degree in English and a master's in education, all paid for by Uncle Sam. Ely Juaregui took responsibility for his own education, and now he's doing everything he can to encourage young people to do the same. He's an absolute inspiration, another in a long line of educators whom students are really blessed to have standing before them in the front of the classroom.

The structure is in place. The key is getting students to see that it's there. How do we do that? If I were philosopher king, my first mandate would be that every parent would be a Wil Colom and a Dorothy Colom— parents who instill an unquenchable love of learning in their children. But I'm not philosopher king, and that's not reality. What is reality is that all parents aren't always as engaged as they could be, and neither are all children. I start every one of my assemblies by talking not about success, but about just the opposite: failure. I talk about going into a prison and finding out that the common denominator among the inmates, in addition to committing a crime, is they can't read. I talk about 85 percent of juveniles placed in detention facilities cannot read. But the problem isn't the system. The problem is someone didn't light the fire of learning under these people when it mattered.

Of course, it's still easy to get discouraged about American education if you look too long in the wrong direction. Not long after my visit to Ely Juaregui's school, I was invited to another California school to speak to fifty recently arrived immigrants from Mexico and Central America about literacy and becoming self-starting autodidactics. I had to give my presentation in Spanish because no one spoke English. These were all eighth-graders. I asked each of them to stand up and tell me where they came from, and how long they'd been here. I remember one kid, from El Salvador, who had been in the country just two weeks. None had been in America more than a year.

The teacher had a list of English words on the wall they were supposed to study, words like *door* and *light* and *book,* the kinds of words you'd find in a first-grade class. As I spoke, what became absolutely clear to me is that there was no way any of these kids would acquire the English skills they needed to go to high school in another year. It is simply not possible to make up eight years of schooling in one year. They were already on a path to failure. High school would have little meaning for them other than as a place to be for six hours each day.

As far as I know, there is no program designed to address this problem. This is the problem nobody wants to talk about. Until it's addressed, there will be no increase in the literacy rates in America.

As the masses get larger, educating them gets harder. In his book *The Knowledge Deficit,* E. D. Hirsch, Jr. makes the point that of all developed nations America has by far the most mobility among its schoolchildren. According to census statistics, every year some twenty million students between the ages of five and fourteen change their residence. That means that one third of the students in an average American school, and anywhere from one half to nearly all of the students in a lower-income inner-city school, will transfer during the school year. No less than one sixth of American third graders will have attended at least three schools by the time they get there.

That kind of mobility does not lend itself to seamless, effective education. Nor is it encouraging to note that in the United States the school year is 180 days long. In South Korea, the number is 220. Japanese kids attend school 242 days each year.

What is the solution? To me, a giant step in the right direction would be to have our schools in session twelve months out of the year. Don't close them for the summer. Don't close them ever. Students need breaks, sure, but three months a year? Particularly when you look at the disastrous effects of the summer slide, causing kids to play catch-up every fall when they return to the classroom.

If we concentrated our resources from prekindergarten to sixth grade and went to year-round school, think of the advantages for our children and our country. And, for that matter, for our teachers, who would now be paid for twelve months' work instead of nine.

But until such a system exists somewhere other than as a fantasy in my brain, it remains imperative that we emphasize the need for our students to be self-starters when it comes to their education, inside the classroom or out. Students who acquire a true affection for learning and literacy will not be dissuaded by transferring to a school in a new city or spending fewer days in the classroom than their counterparts in Japan. Boundaries disappear for autodidacts. Horizons are limitless for readers and learners.

I like what the novelist Edmund White said about reading: "Reading was a magical portal—once you passed through it, you couldn't even imagine going back."

And this one: "Quite concretely, reading has always struck me as a passport to the world, one in which characters are more real than actual people, where values are more intense than in the dim light of reality, where characters fly up into destinies rather than paddle around in ambiguity."

I've always loved this passage from the novel *Stoner* by John Williams: "Sometimes, immersed in his books, there would come to him the awareness of all he didn't know, of all he had not read; and the serenity for which he labored was shattered, as he realized the little time he had left in life to read so much, to learn what he had to know."

Those statements resonate with me deeply because of my own personal love affair with reading and literature. In my home there are 1,474 books, and I have read every one of them. I can't fully explain what that means to me personally. Reading has taken me to places I'd never have gone, introduced me to characters I'd never have known. I've been to sea in World War II; I've sat in Uncle Tom's cabin and ridden in a pickup truck with Tom Joad and stood in the thick of Civil War battles. I can sit down on a fourteen-hour flight, and it goes by lightning fast if I've got one thing: a good book. Books don't put me to sleep; they wake me up, they excite me, they make me think through issues I never even knew were out there.

What better way to spend an evening than reading *Gone with the Wind* or *To Kill a Mockingbird* or *The Grapes of Wrath* or a great biography? Pull out *The Caine Mutiny* by Herman Wouk and read pages sixty-three to sixty-six. I can remember to this day where I was when I read those passages, and how they stopped me in my tracks with their clarity and their beauty. The characters are fictitious, but the sentiment is true. That is one of the beauties and blessings of books. They help us understand this journey we call life.

I feel the same way about writing. Being able to express how I feel with the written word is enormously liberating and empowering. Writing gives life to my thoughts, giving them a timelessness and importance well beyond those of the spoken word. Things endure when they're written down. They *matter*. I think of Anne Frank. She was as alone as alone can be, shut up in an attic, unable to speak above a whisper, in constant fear for her life. Her only recourse was her diary. It was her confidant, her unwavering companion, when she had no other. I don't think it's possible for us to fully comprehend the solace it gave that teenage girl to be able to chronicle her experiences while hiding from the Nazis, any more than we can completely comprehend how much good her words have done for the world. Untold millions have read the words of Anne Frank and been both appalled and inspired by them.

What we write becomes history, a record, a lasting document, a voice. The more I write, I find, the more I want to write. I want to expand my vocabulary so I can express myself more succinctly.

Then there's the practical value of vocabulary and writing. Want a good job? Want to get a promotion? Want to impress someone? Want to win an argument? Writing is your ticket to all of the above. If you can't write, you'll never have an idea in your head that you can defend.

Throughout history, those in control have known that literacy is the key to power. Those with it, rule. Those without it, don't. Consider the history of one of America's most celebrated (and unfortunately tragic) families: the Kennedys. The clan's roots trace back to Ireland, where living conditions in the early 1800s were so wretched that parents routinely put their children on a boat for America, with the distinct prospect that they would never see them again. But when the dirt-poor forebears of John F. Kennedy set sail for the new world, they did not go unarmed. They carried with them an ability to read and write—skills they had acquired surreptitiously at so-called hedge schools. These hedge schools were against the law and operated out of sight, typically in ditches or hedges alongside roadways. Catholic priests and other educated people would act as the instructors. As Robert F. Kennedy, Jr. points out in his book *American Values*, the priest who had taught his ancestors was discovered, found guilty in a court of law, and hanged for the offense.

Once in their new home, the Kennedys found a much more inclusive freedom in the world's emerging incubator of democracy. Scorned and ridiculed at first, it wasn't long before they expanded their education and became successful and prosperous.

Of course, even in America, it hasn't always been easy. My thoughts circle back to the Shiloh battlefield in Tennessee, where this book began, and to Andrew Jackson Smith, a man born an illiterate slave whose great-great-grandchildren are educated beyond anything he could have ever imagined.

The Andy Smith story encapsulates for me what is most wonderful about education in America and what is most dangerous.

On the one hand, as the Civil War long ago indelibly established, ours is a country that recognizes that every person, without exception, is free to become literate and learned. It is precisely why we have a public school system open to all.

On the other hand, the freedom we treasure does not guarantee literacy and learning to anyone. The system is useless if it is not utilized. I look at statistics from Detroit, where in 2015, 93 percent of eighth graders were considered not proficient in reading, and it's just heartbreaking. A majority of them are African Americans. I find myself wondering what Andy Smith would make of that.

My nagging fear is not so much that we're losing ground, but that we'll keep losing ground.

Too many kids in America—too many people of all ages—can't read and write as well as they need to. That's our problem. Like all problems, it can get better or it can get worse.

My resolve is to continue the fight to make it better. I'm blessed beyond belief to be able to do what I'm doing. Many sponsors have stepped up along the way to help pay the way. They've looked at what I'm trying to accomplish and have provided the funding and support that allows me to continue to tilt at windmills.

Unlike me, almost all of them wish to remain anonymous, completely off the stage. But I know who they are, and they know who they are, and I will be forever in their debt.

In my "second career," I am free to walk the greatest country on earth and encourage people to read and write and learn.

Does everyone listen? Not by a long shot. But some do, such as the young man who sent me this letter (I've changed the name of the student and school for reasons of privacy):

October 5. 2016

Dear Mr. Parkinson:

Hello my name is Chase Jackson, and I am currently a sophomore at Warm Springs High School. I am a 15 year old student athlete. I read your book Autodidactic and it is people like you that inspire people like me. I was in the front row when you looked me in the eyes and smiled and said you are important. I know you had no idea what I was going through at the time, but I had just got out of the biggest struggles of my life.

One of my biggest struggles in life was being in foster care. The reason I think foster care was a big struggle for me is because you have to find a way to survive. I had two choices, I could come home to a stranger or I could live on a street that I knew too well. I was always looking for a someone to call Dad or Mom and It hurt me a lot. I don't even know what my Mom or Dad look like. It was hard and people said I wouldn't make it. At one point I thought I wouldn't. I couldn't even look at myself in the mirror. I saw failure and hate. Something inside me didn't want that. No matter how far success was inside me I could see it and I wanted it. Now I'm closer than ever and nothing is going to stop me, because I have the support at home and at school and I have a Dad like I always wanted. "Your scars are just memories of how the world tried to break you and failed". Your book inspired me to face my challenges head on and realize that no matter where someone comes from or what they look like you can succeed.

Honestly going into your presentation before you even talked I thought it was going to be pointless. But as soon as you told me I'm worth something you changed my life. I stopped and thought after you were done talking and thought I want to change many people's lives just like this man has with his book and his speeches. I don't want to win any money. All I want is for you to know that you are important to the world and you have made a difference in the world.

Sincerely,
Chase Jackson

It was Henry David Thoreau who said, "To have made one person's life a little better, that is to succeed."

That remains my mantra.

My hope for Chase Jackson, and all the others out there like him, is they will realize their importance and carve their own valuable niche, using the tool of education to help them do so.

BIBLIOGRAPHY

Abadzi, Helen. *Efficient Learning for the Poor: Insights from the Frontier of Cognitive Neuroscience.* Washington, DC: World Bank, 2006.

Anders, George. *The Rare Find: How Great Talent Stands Out.* New York: Portfolio/ Penguin, 2012.

Andersen, Richard. *Powerful Writing Skills.* New York: Fall River Press, 2001.

Bauerlein, Mark. *The Dumbest Generation: How the Digital Age Stupifies Young Americans and Jeopardizes Our Future (or, Don't Trust Anyone Under 30).* New York: Penguin, 2008.

Baumeister, Roy F., and John Tierney. *Willpower: Rediscovering the Greatest Human Strength.* New York: Penguin Books, 2012.

Benjamin, Aaron S., and Robert A. Bjork. *Successful Remembering and Successful Forgetting: A Festschrift in Honor of Robert A. Bjork.* London ; New York: Routledge, Taylor Et Francis Group, 2016.

Bennett, Alan. *The Uncommon Reader.* New York: Picador, 2008.

Bloom, Benjamin S., and Lauren A. Sosniak. *Developing Talent in Young People.* New York: Ballantine, 1988.

Bolton, Charles C. *The Hardest Deal of All: The Battle Over School Integration in Mississippi, 1870-1980.* Jackson, MS: University Press of Mississippi, 2005.

Brown, Peter C. *Make It Stick: The Science of Successful Learning.* Cambridge, MA: Belknap Harvard, 2018.

Carey, Benedict. *How We Learn: The Surprising Truth about When, Where and Why It Happens.* New York: Random House, 2015.

Christensen, Clayton M., and Henry J. Eyring. *The Innovative University: Changing the DNA of Higher Education from the Inside Out.* San Francisco: Jossey-Bass A Wiley Imprint, 2011.

Chua, Amy. *Battle Hymn of the Tiger Mother.* New York: Penguin Press, 2011.

Collins, Jim. *Good to Great: Why Some Companies Make the Leap ... and Others Don't.* New York: Harper Business, 2001.

Colvin, Geoffrey. *Talent Is Overrated: What Really Separates World-class Performers from Everybody Else.* New York: Portfolio/Penguin, 2018.

Coyle, Daniel. *The Talent Code: Greatness Isn't Born: It's Grown, Here's How.* New York: Bantam Books, 2009.

Coyle, Daniel. *The Little Book of Talent: 52 Tips for Improving Your Skills.* New York: Bantam Books, 2012.

Currey, Mason. *Daily Rituals: How Artists Work.* New York: Alfred A. Knopf, 2016.

Darder, Antonia. *Reinventing Paulo Freire: A Pedagogy of Love.* New York: London: Routledge, 2017.

Dehaene, Stanislas. *Reading in the Brain: The Science and Evolution of a Human Invention.* New York: Penguin Books, 2010.

DeMille, Oliver Van, and Sharon Brooks. *Thomas Jefferson Education for Teens.* Cedar City, UT: TJEdOnline, 2009.

DeMille, Oliver Van. *A Thomas Jefferson Education: Teaching a Generation of Leaders for the Twenty-first Century.* Cedar City, UT: Thomas Jefferson Education, 2017.

Deresiewicz, William. *Excellent Sheep: The Miseducation of the American Elite and the Way to a Meaningful Life.* New York: Free Press, 2015.

Didau, David. *The Secret of Literacy: Making the Implicit Explicit.* Bancyfelin: Independent Thinking Press, 2014.

Didau, David, Robert A. Bjork, and Dylan Wiliam. *What If Everything You Knew about Education Was Wrong?* Wales: Crown House Publishing, 2016.

Doidge, Norman. *The Brain That Changes Itself: Stories of Personal Triumph from the Frontiers of Brain Science.* Melbourne: Scribe, 2010.

Douglass, Frederick, and Harriet Jacobs. *Narrative of the Life of Frederick Douglass, an American Slave and Incidents In the Life of a Slave Girl.* St. Louis, MO: San Val, 2000.

Douglass, Frederick, Kwame Anthony Appiah, and Harriet Ann Jacobs. *Narrative of the Life of Frederick Douglass, an American Slave.* New York: Modern Library, 2004.

Duckworth, Angela. *Grit: The Power of Passion and Perseverance.* New York: Scribner, 2018.

Duhigg, Charles. *The Power of Habit: Why We Do What We Do, and How to Change.* New York: Random House, 2012.

Dweck, Carol S. *Mindset: The New Psychology of Success.* New York, NY: Random House, 2016.

Ellsberg, Michael. *The Education of Millionaires: Everything You Won't Learn in College about How to Be Successful.* New York: Portfolio/Penguin, 2012.

Engelmann, Siegfried. *War against the Schools Academic Child Abuse.* Portland, OR: Halcyon House, 1992.

Ericsson, Karl Anders, and Robert Pool. *Peak: Secrets from the New Science of Expertise.* London: Bodley Head, 2016.

Bibliography

Espy, Willard R. *Words at Play: Palindromes, Riddles, Malapropisms, and Other Wonderful Word Games.* New York: Tess Press, 2007.

Foer, Joshua. *Moonwalking with Einstein: A Journey through Memory and the Mind.* London: Allen Lane, 2011.

Franklin, Benjamin, and Leonard Woods. *The Autobiography of Benjamin Franklin.* New Haven, CT: Yale University Press, 1964.

Gallagher, Kelly, and Richard L. Allington. *Readicide: How Schools Are Killing Reading and What You Can Do about It.* Portland, ME: Stenhouse Publishers, 2009.

Gallo, Carmine. *Talk like TED: The 9 Public-Speaking Secrets of the Worlds Top Minds.* New York: St. Martins Griffin, 2015.

Gatto, John Taylor. *Dumbing Us Down: The Hidden Curriculum of Compulsory Schooling.* Philadelphia: New Society Publishers, 2002.

Gilovich, Thomas. *How We Know What Isn't So: The Fallibility of Human Reason in Everyday Life.* New York: Free Press, 1991.

Gladwell, Malcolm. *Outliers.* New York: Little, Brown and Company, 2008.

Gladwell, Malcolm. *Blink: The Power of Thinking without Thinking.* New York: Back Bay Books, 2013.

Gladwell, Malcolm. *The Tipping Point: How Little Things Can Make a Big Difference.* New York: Little, Brown & Company, 2013.

Gladwell, Malcolm. *David and Goliath Underdogs, Misfits, and the Art of Battling Giants.* New York: Back Bay Books, 2015.

Gottlieb, Robert. *Avid Reader: A Life.* New York: Picador, 2017.

Green, Elizabeth. *Building a Better Teacher: How Teaching Works (and How to Teach It to Everyone).* New York: W.W. Norton & Company, 2015.

Hallowell, Edward M., and John J. Ratey. *Driven to Distraction: Recognizing and Coping with Attention Deficit Disorder from Childhood through Adulthood.* New York: Anchor Books, 2011.

Hart, Betty, and Todd R. Risley. *Meaningful Differences: Everyday Parenting and Intellectual Development in Young American Children.* Baltimore: Paul H. Brookes, 1995.

Hallowell, Edward M., and John J. Ratey. *Driven to Distraction: Recognizing and Coping with Attention Deficit Disorder from Childhood through Adulthood.* New York: Simon & Schuster, 1994.

Hart, Betty. *Meaningful Differences in the Everyday Experience of Young American Children.* Baltimore: Brookes Publishing, 1995.

Hess, Frederick M. *The Same Thing Over and Over: How School Reformers Get Stuck in Yesterday's Ideas.* Cambridge, MA: Harvard University Press, 2010.

Heuston, Dustin Hull., and James W. Parkinson. *The Third Source: a Message of Hope for Education.* Salt Lake City, UT: Dustin Hull Heuston, 2011.

Hirsch, E. D. *The Knowledge Deficit: Creating a Reading Revolution for a New Generation of American Achievers.* New York: Houghton Mifflin, 2006.

Kahneman, Daniel. *Thinking, Fast and Slow.* New York: Farrar, Straus and Giroux, 2011.

Kaufman, Scott Barry. *Ungifted: Intelligence Redefined.* New York: Basic Books, 2013.

Kilpatrick, James Jackson. *The Writer's Art.* Kansas City, MO: Andrews, McMeel & Parker, 1984.

King, Stephen. *On Writing: a Memoir of the Craft.* New York: Scribner, 2000.

Kuo, Michelle. *Reading with Patrick: a Teacher, a Student, and a Life-Changing Friendship.* New York: Macmillan, 2017.

L'Amour, Louis. *Education of a Wandering Man.* New York: Bantam, 2008.

Lester, Mark, and Larry Beason. *The McGraw-Hill Handbook of English Grammar and Usage.* New York: McGraw-Hill, 2005.

Macedo, Donaldo P. *Literacies of Power: What Americans Are Not Allowed to Know.* Boulder, CO: Westview Press, 2006.

Medina, John. *Brain Rules: 12 Principles for Surviving and Thriving at Work, Home, and School.* Seattle: Pear Press, 2008.

Michener, James A. *The World Is My Home: a Memoir.* New York: Random House, 1992.

Miller, Donalyn. *The Book Whisperer: Awakening the Inner Reader in Every Child.* San Francisco Jossey-Bass, 2009.

Moyers, Bill. *Fooling with Words: a Celebration of Poets and Their Craft.* New York: Perennial, 1999.

Nasaw, David. *Andrew Carnegie.* New York: Penguin, 2007.

Nater, Swen, and Ronald Gallimore. *You Haven't Taught until They Have Learned: John Wooden's Teaching Principles and Practices.* Dexter, MI: Thomson-Shore Inc., 2006.

Nisbett, Richard E. *Intelligence and How to Get It: Why Schools and Cultures Count.* New York: W.W. Norton & Co, 2010.

Pennebaker, James W. *The Secret Life of Pronouns: What Our Words Say about Us.* New York: Bloomsbury Press, 2011.

Pinker, Steven. *How the Mind Works.* New York: W.W. Norton, 2009.

Prose, Francine. *Reading like a Writer: A Guide for People Who Love Books and for Those Who Want to Write Them.* New York: HarperCollins Publishers, 2007.

Ravitch, Diane. *Reign of Error.* New York: Alfred A. Knopf, 2013.

Ravitch, Diane. *The Death and Life of the Great American School System: How Testing and Choice Are Undermining Education.* New York: Basic Books, 2010.

Bibliography

Ravitch, Diane. *The Language Police: How Pressure Groups Restrict What Students Learn.* New York: Vintage Books, 2004.

Rhee, Michelle. *Radical: Fighting to Put Students First.* New York: Harper, 2013.

Ripley, Amanda. *The Smartest Kids in the World and How They Got That Way.* New York: Simon & Schuster, 2014.

Roth, Michael S. *Beyond the University: Why Liberal Education Matters.* New Haven, CT: Yale University Press, 2015.

Schacter, Daniel L. *The Seven Sins of Memory: How the Mind Forgets and Remembers.* New York: Houghton Mifflin, 2001.

Schulz, Kathryn. *Being Wrong Adventures in the Margin of Error.* New York: Harper Collins, 2010.

Shaw, Harry. *Punctuate It Right!* New York: HarperPerennial, 1993.

Shenk, David. *The Genius in All of Us: New Insights into Genetics, Talent, and IQ.* New York: Doubleday, 2010.

Stevenson, Harold W., and James W. Stigler. *The Learning Gap: Why Our Schools Are failing and What We Can Learn from Japanese and Chinese Education.* New York: Simon & Schuster Paperbacks, 2006.

Strunk, William. *The Elements of Style.* Boston: Allyn & Bacon, 2000.

Taggart, Caroline, and J. A. Wines. *My Grammar and I: or Should That Be Me?: How to Speak and Write It Right.* New York: Houghton The Reader's Digest Association, Inc., 2014.

Tarkenton, Fran. *The Power of Failure: Succeeding in the Age of Innovation.* Washington, DC: Regnery Publishing, 2015.

Tough, Paul. *How Children Succeed: Grit, Curiosity, and the Hidden Power of Character.* New York: Houghton Mifflin Harcourt, 2013.

Tough, Paul. *Whatever It Takes: Geoffrey Canada's Quest to Change Harlem and America.* New York: Houghton Mifflin, 2008.

Trimble, John R. *Writing with Style: Conversations on the Art of Writing.* Upper Saddle River, NJ: Prentice Hall, 2000.

Truss, Lynne. *Eats, Shoots & Leaves: The Zero Tolerance Approach to Punctuation.* London: Fourth Estate, 2009.

Westover, Tara. *Educated: A Memoir.* New York: Random House, 2018.

Williams, Heather Andrea. *Self-Taught: African American Education in Slavery and Freedom.* Chapel Hill, NC: The University of North Carolina Press, 2005.

Williams, John. *Stoner.* New York: New York Review Books, 1965.

Willingham, Daniel T. *Raising Kids Who Read: What Parents and Teachers Can Do.* San Francisco: Jossey-Bass & Pfeiffer Imprints, Wiley, 2015.

Wolff, Daniel J. *How Lincoln Learned to Read: Twelve Great Americans and the Educations That Made Them.* New York: Bloomsbury, 2010.

Wood, John. *Creating Room to Read: a Story of Hope in the Battle for Global Literacy.* New York: Penguin Group, 2014.

X, Malcolm, and Alex Haley. *The Autobiography of Malcolm X.* New York: Penguin Ballantine Books, 1964.

Zakaria, Fareed. *In Defense of a Liberal Education.* New York: Penguin W. W. Norton & Company, 2016.